JONATHAN BRADLEY is the rugby correspondent at the *Belfast Telegraph* and the creator of the *Ulster Rugby Round-up* podcast. Covering the sport since 2014, he has also written for the *Rugby Paper, Irish Independent, Irish Times* and *Sunday Independent. The Last Amateurs* is his first book. He lives in Belfast with his wife, Christina.

The Last Amateurs

The Incredible Story of
ULSTER RUGBY'S
1999 EUROPEAN
CHAMPIONS

JONATHAN BRADLEY

·THE·
BLACK
·STAFF·
PRESS

For my mum and dad, who always encouraged
a love of sport and a love of books, even if not
necessarily at the same time.

First published in 2018 by Blackstaff Press
an imprint of Colourpoint Creative Ltd, Colourpoint House,
Jubilee Business Park, 21 Jubilee Road,
Newtownards, BT23 4YH

© Text, Jonathan Bradley, 2018

Printed in Berwick-upon-Tweed by Martins the Printers

A CIP catalogue for this book is available from the British Library

ISBN 978-1-78073-181-0

www.blackstaffpress.com

CONTENTS

PROLOGUE

9.30 a.m., 30 January 1999

The man with the keys to Lansdowne Road is adamant that, for all he knows, Simon Mason could be an imposter.

Mason's face has been everywhere since Ulster booked their place in this afternoon's European Cup final thanks to an incredible win over French powerhouse Stade Français three weeks ago. Interest in Ulster has mushroomed since that most unlikely of results and, with the country captivated, members of the media from far and wide have been seeking out the province's adopted Liverpudlian, who has kicked this unheralded bunch to the verge of being crowned Ireland's first-ever European champions.

Not that you'd know it from the scene unfolding at the gates of the famous old stadium, where this morning's kicking practice can't get underway until key meets lock. As trains rumble past, ferrying some forty thousand Ulster fans into Dublin, all with their hopes resting on Mason's right boot, the stadium attendant continues to argue that the twenty-five-year-old star could just be any one of the horde arriving early without a ticket and chancing his luck.

Head-to-toe in Ulster gear, in the days when such tracksuits were still a luxury for the players, and were definitely not items available to any fan wandering into a club shop, it seems unlikely that Mason isn't who he says he is, but the only man whose opinion matters sticks to his guns. Ever affable backs coach, Colin Wilkinson, draws distractedly on one of his Benson & Hedges as even he struggles to keep his cool. He hopes this unforeseen hitch won't knock Mason off his stride on the very day Ulster need him most. Soon enough, he'll have no such worries.

Team doctor David Irwin, who himself represented Ireland with distinction for a decade, as well as touring with the British and Irish Lions, could perhaps take most offence at the notion that they're a trio of interlopers looking to sneak into the stadium some five hours early, but he manages to hold his tongue.

Ironically, Mason had no such problems getting into Irish Rugby HQ the day before. He and his room-mate, reserve scrum half Stephen Bell, had ambled round from the Berkeley Court Hotel, and simply hopped over a fence.

As dusk had descended on Dublin, the pair had sat in the south stand and thought of the coming day. Mason – who grew up aspiring to be the next Kenny Dalglish: scoring goals not kicking points – daydreamed of the sea of red that would greet the teams as they ran out, a similar sight to the one that must have greeted his Liverpool heroes at Anfield on the magical European nights he remembered from the 1980s.

Harry Williams, former Holywood Primary School headmaster turned pro rugby coach, had believed his side's name was on the trophy since their stunning win over Toulouse in the quarter-finals. His players were now daring to think the same. Mason imagined holding the cup aloft, giving Ulster's fairy tale the happy ending that had seemed beyond improbable when the side, as was the norm, had staggered through the early rounds. He pictured himself kicking the winning points, proving once and for all that he'd been discarded far too early by the national selectors, and bringing back silverware for the troubled province that had so quickly felt like home when he'd arrived from

Liverpool just six months ago.

Today, though, things weren't proving quite as straightforward as they had been in his head.

'No ID, I can't let you in,' maintained the attendant, sounding more and more like a bouncer on the door of a pub.

Jobsworth, Mason thought to himself. Still, just hours away from the biggest game of his life, he remained remarkably serene. Reminiscing some years later, he said he'd since wondered if the world's top sportsmen, the likes of Messi and Ronaldo, spent every game of their careers feeling the way he did that winter's day in Dublin. For now, though, he just appreciated the assurance surging through his veins that had been there since he'd woken up that morning, lying in the very same hotel room he'd occupied when he'd made his Ireland debut three years before. It was the hunt for more international caps that had ultimately led him here, but now he chased a different dream.

He'd been in incredible form since he'd first stepped off the Liverpool boat, taking little note of those who had questioned why anyone would choose to move to a city still scarred by three decades of the Troubles, let alone take a 50 per cent pay cut for the privilege. He'd always felt more comfortable in an Ulster jersey than a high-spending Richmond one, where a day kicking from the tee yielding nine from ten would still bring questions about the lone miss. At Ulster, they were all in it together, even if it was he who got the plaudits, thanks to his metronome of a kicking stroke.

It didn't change the pressures, though; not when the hush descended and he approached the kicking tee. He always felt that sickness before big games, imagining being handed a kick from the sideline and watching in horror as it lifted only five metres off the ground, like an injured bird trying to take flight, before returning to the turf. Before the semi against the best side in France, Stade Français, he was wracked with nerves, even as teammates around him somehow talked themselves into believing a historic victory was imminent. With a game plan designed specifically to win penalties for him to knock over, he was always aware of the need to capitalise on his teammates' hard work. Mason, ye daft eejit, he'd imagined Justin Fitzpatrick saying, should he be wayward with a straightforward penalty won by the loose head prop's destructive scrummaging. Kicking when stakes are at their highest is a skill he's always seen as similar to playing blackjack – there are no grey areas. Succeed and you're a hero; fail and you feel like the worst in the world.

Since arriving in Ulster, it seemed he'd been beating the dealer whether he chose to stick or twist, but he still turned white at the thought of his talents deserting him when he needed them most. But not today in Dublin. Today Mason has utter confidence in his ability. The idea that this final could end with Colomiers lifting the trophy doesn't enter his head.

But first he has to get into the stadium. Finally, he reaches a compromise with the attendant and the trio, along with a sack of size five Gilberts, are allowed on to the side pitch at Lansdowne Road. Better late than never, the morning practice can begin.

In preparation, balls are placed at six different spots along the twenty-two while Mason readies himself for a routine he's carried out at least every other day of his entire adult life.

When he'd initially practised with Colin Wilkinson, shortly after his first team training session at Ravenhill back in July, Wilkinson had been so impressed he'd said that Mason was already far too good a kicker to learn anything from the likes of him. But if the post-training kicking that day was eye-catching, it was nothing compared to Mason's form on the morning of the biggest match of his life.

As Wilkinson continued to place balls, he heard a familiar clang. Mason was standing on the try line taking aim at the uprights, the theory being that if you can aim for and hit one of the posts, then putting it between them should pose relatively

4

few problems. Another clang, then another. The sound echoed through the empty stands and told Wilkinson all he needed to know.

Moving back to the twenty-two, and starting on the right, Mason methodically begins to replicate his penalty goal stroke, the one practised thousands and thousands of times: head down and follow through. With Wilkinson looking on in amazement, the first twenty-nine balls all fly between the posts with a precision that suggests there wasn't ever any alternative.

As Mason lines up one final kick, his thoughts drift back to his very first steps in the game. He's six years old again, occupying himself at Birkenhead Park while his father finishes up at a committee meeting inside. Without a witness, few would have believed that the young Mason could have booted the ball over and between the posts, and no one could have known that it was the first of what would be a career's worth of such feats.

When he next places the ball on the tee, a lack of witnesses won't be a problem, not with forty-nine thousand crammed to the rafters of Lansdowne Road and hanging on his every kick. He puts that thought to one side as he concludes his routine, striking the last ball sweetly and watching it scythe through the crisp Dublin air like scissors through paper.

Straight between the posts. Again.

No, nothing is going to go wrong here, he reassures himself. It's going to be our day.

1
A RUDE AWAKENING

Ulster's worst day in Europe produced something of an out-of-body experience for Andy Matchett.

There are few more thankless tasks in rugby than that of a run-of-the-mill back rower chasing down a quick scrum half – bearing stark similarities to how Wile E. Coyote must have felt chasing Road Runner – always getting just close enough to feel him blow past the despairing tackle, the faintest touch of fingertip on jersey a painful reminder of how 'close' counts for little in sport.

The problem for Matchett on the afternoon of 21 September 1997 was that Lawrence Dallaglio was anything but run of the mill. At six feet four inches tall, with well north of seventeen stone behind him in the tackle, the Wasps number eight didn't so much chase half backs as hunt them down. Clad in the traditional black of the then London club, the victorious Lion and soon-to-be England captain looked every inch the assassin as he drove Ulstermen into the Loftus Road turf time and time again.

When Matchett peered up from another ruck in a game that was quickly unravelling, time seemed to slow down. Bracing for impact, it was as if he could see the collision coming from above, as if he was watching a misfortune befalling somebody else. Look at the size of Dallaglio, he thought to himself. Thwack. As the collision thundered through his body like a car crash, he shuddered back to reality.

When Matchett had first represented the province, it was

Ulster that had struck fear into the opposition, not the other way around. He had made his debut in the early nineties, when Ulster's rugby team was the pride of Ireland. Back then, learning your trade at Ravenhill was the equivalent of an Ivy League education.

'It was a really strong side and I was the young kid on the block at that stage,' Matchett recalls. 'I always remember Willie Anderson saying, "You just get the ball out to Peter Russell and that'll do us." That's all I was trying to do. We went down to Thomond Park and beat Munster, and I remember at half-time they'd kicked the life out of Davy Irwin, the way you can't do any more. There was plenty of mouthing, too – you had the likes of Peter Clohessy in that Munster team, so there was no holding back. Davy Irwin wouldn't have been a popular character down there. He and Willie Anderson, they were both quite in your face, shall we say. Davy was in there ranting, "Look at what these fuckers have done to me!" I was twenty-one years old, sat in the corner wondering what I was doing in this madhouse getting my shit kicked in. But we ended up winning – that's the way it seemed to go back then.'

By 1997, times had changed.

Ulster, who had earned at the very least a share of every interprovincial title between 1985 and 1994, had become a different team in the years since. By the time the sport staggered into professionalism, and the inaugural Heineken Cup began in 1995, the side's decade of dominance was already the subject of misty-eyed nostalgia. The feats of David Irwin, Trevor Ringland, Nigel Carr, Keith Crossan and Willie Anderson, men who formed the spine of the greatest team to ever call Ravenhill home, were memories. How that team would have done in a European Cup wasn't really a question on the terraces in Belfast, for that would have implied some sort of debate surrounding the topic. That they'd have won it three or four times over was an unquestioned truth so oft repeated that younger generations would be forgiven for thinking they had done just that, that gathering dust somewhere were pictures of those players hoisting silverware after vanquishing the very best that the rugby-playing world had to offer.

Their successors – those who finally saw the vice-like grip on the interprovincial series loosened and who would be the first to represent the nine counties in the newly formed cross-continental competition – were not of the same ilk. The early days of Ulster in Europe wasn't a case of David versus Goliath, instead it was more akin to the Christians thrown to the lions. Seven losses in their first eight games left little room for argument: Ulster and the glamour tournament were uneasy bedfellows. And that was before they ran into Wasps.

There are times when, muddling your way through a situation, the fact that you have reached the nadir only becomes clear afterwards; a moment of clarity later bringing the realisation that that was indeed rock bottom. On other occasions, when faced with straits so dire that it's impossible to avoid the obvious conclusion, you can sense a low as it's playing out in front of you. It was a case of the latter the day Ulster travelled to Loftus Road to meet Dallaglio and Co. and were not just beaten but annihilated.

While losing in Europe was nothing new to the side – it was par for the course since the night there had been forty points between them and Cardiff in their very first game – confronting the glitz and allure of English giants in a spacious football ground and coming out on the wrong end of a 56–3 battering made one thing abundantly clear: the gap between the Ulstermen and the Wasps of this world was getting wider and wider. Sooner or later it would be impossible to bridge. With a makeshift backline, a largely amateur squad and a wholly amateur attitude, the difference between the haves and have nots competing in the same competition was as pronounced as it would ever be.

Even while Wasps rested the likes of Simon Shaw and Andy

Gomarsall, they could still field a fifteen that included Dallaglio and the great Scot Kenny Logan, the wing who grabbed the headlines on that September day, scoring three of his side's eight tries. All their players were paid, and handsomely so, considering such dealings had belonged in grubby brown envelopes as recently as 1995. Meanwhile Ulster had only five pro players on the standard Irish Rugby Football Union (IRFU) contract of the time: 25,000 Irish punts a year along with a car. Fresh from a victorious Lions tour in South Africa, and only months away from his first Test as England captain, Dallaglio would soon be making more than ten times that amount when endorsement deals were taken into consideration. These were two sides existing on different planes.

The game had actually started encouragingly for Ulster. After half an hour, the score was knotted at 3–3: out-half Stuart Laing's penalty had ensured an even footing as half-time approached. The issue came when the hosts scored the game's final fifty-three points. Shane Roiser and Simon Mitchell both grabbed tries before half-time and the difference between the sides was hammered home after the turn as an increasingly ragged Ulster side was torn asunder by Wasps' incisive backs and Logan's hat-trick of tries scored in just eleven minutes in the second half.

'As if the half-century of points were not enough of a gulf, by the end Wasps showed that in terms of fitness and nous they are light years ahead,' wrote David Llewellyn in his match report for the *Independent*. It wasn't an assertion contested by Ulster who had begun to adopt professionalism in that most stereotypically Irish of ways – a job to be undertaken slowly and to be completed whenever they got around to it.

Among the small rank of paid players on the visiting side was Jan Cunningham, who had put his legal career on hold to chase the dream of being a full-time rugby player. While it would be seven years before he returned to the hard graft of law, his early rugby forays were hardly labour intensive. Without even enough bodies for a game of five-a-side, he and the other salaried players would congregate for a gym session in the morning and then be left to kill the day with PlayStation or golf until the working majority of the squad were ready for training in the evening.

'It was bizarre,' remembers Cunningham, whose younger brother Bryn made the first of his 150 Ulster outings from the bench in the game. 'We knew then that in the European Cup … the other teams were professional and we weren't. We played Wasps, full-time professionals, and the only concessions we had made to it were four guys turning up to do weight sessions. We were behind the curve. It was a hiding at the time but that scoreline – it was the equivalent of having eighty or ninety put on you nowadays. I think I touched the ball once and it was a knock-on. You just thought "What are we doing here? We're not in the same league." We were so far behind, it was a farce. They were professional. We were too, but in name not nature.'

While the Premiership giant's star names had designs on being the very best, whether that be in Europe or on the national stage, where Clive Woodward was two years into a rebuild with England that would eventually yield a World Cup, Ulster's aims were certainly more modest in the face of odds that seemed insurmountable. They had gone into that 1997–98 season with Royal Belfast Academical Institution schoolmaster Davy Haslett at the helm – a man who balanced a host of representative coaching experience at an underage level with teaching geography, and who came to the Ulster job only after a long-running saga.

Birkenhead-born Tony Russ had become the province's first paid coach back in August 1996, signing a cut-price deal worth £35,000 a year following an abrupt sacking after a successful stint in charge of the Leicester Tigers. His time at Ravenhill was short-lived, however, and he was lured back across the Irish Sea by Waterloo. The promise of an extra fifteen grand a season and the same amount available in bonuses was cited as the motivating factor for the move, but Russ, who would ultimately leave the Liverpool-based club to run a guesthouse in the Lake District, was known to be perturbed that after a season in which his team won just two of eight games, it would be six months before he saw his players to prepare for the next campaign, thanks to the pre-eminent status afforded to the clubs in the All-Ireland League.

His successor was to be Clive Griffiths but the Welshman, long thought to be dragging his heels on a deal offered back in April, eventually backed out come the summer, leaving Ulster with nobody. Cue Haslett's appointment. Set to head to New Zealand as assistant coach on Ireland's ill-fated A/Development tour, Haslett was offered the position by Ulster the day before the party left Dublin. This move still had to be given the go-ahead by Irish coach Brian Ashton, who had met with Griffiths in April to discuss strategic planning. Having taken the job in charge of the national side with a guarantee that all four provinces would have full-time coaches in place, Ashton left for the southern hemisphere fuming that Griffiths, as well as John Bevan who had been due to take Munster's helm, had both reneged on their deals. Ashton himself would resign from the top job later that year only twelve months into a six-year contract to be replaced by Warren Gatland, the thirty-four-year-old Kiwi in charge of Connacht.

When the bedraggled Irish party returned from New Zealand, there were just four weeks for Haslett to work with the side before he departed on a pre-booked holiday to Greece, and to make matters worse, a friendly with Glasgow was scrapped after the two sides were paired in the Heineken Cup. As a result, there was only one warm-up fixture before the interpro series began. It was a game against a Richmond side who brought a host of star names to the Palace Grounds in Armagh, including a full back with a magical boot named Simon Mason (presumably he caught the eye). In typical fashion that year, the appointments of Charlie McAleese as assistant coach and John Kinnear as team manager came well after preseason began.

The hastily assembled squad lost to Leinster at Donnybrook before their first defeat at the hands of Connacht in fifteen years. They at least beat Munster 22–10 in Belfast, securing qualification for Europe's top competition in 1998–99 by virtue of points difference over Connacht, even if some out west still doubt Ulster would have been denied their place had they finished bottom of the Irish pile that year. To start they fared little better in Europe, losing to both Glasgow and Swansea in their opening fixtures, so it was little wonder that Ulster travelled to Wasps with low expectations. The trip to London started as you might expect, with a number of pints, and stayed to script with a hammering that two decades later would still stand as the side's record losing margin in continental competition.

That same season Andy Ward became an international, going from representing Ulster in Loftus Road to playing for Ireland against South Africa in Loftus Versfeld just eight short months later, and with three Five Nations' outings in between. But the performance against Wasps left him wondering just how Ulster would look moving forward. In the cramped confines of Loftus Road – a ground somewhat left behind by the Premier League explosion, thanks to QPR's relegation in the spring of 1996 – he was left with little doubt over how far his side had to go if such indignities were ever to cease. 'It was the first time we'd played on a football pitch – with changing rooms designed for eleven footballers not twenty-five rugby players – so we were shoehorned in before kick-off and it was all quite bizarre. We got a humping and it was an eye-opener in terms of how far away we were on so many fronts. We were miles off and needed to get our shit sorted.'

Despite their three losses at the start of the competition, Ulster beat Swansea in the return fixture for their second ever European win and as such – in what was an unusually structured tournament – maintained a slim chance of progressing into a six-team play-off for a quarter-final spot, only to lose to Glasgow and finish bottom of their pool for the second time in three attempts. An average of 3,283 hardy souls turned up to watch their home fixtures in the competition.

The Wasps outfit that taught Ulster so painful a lesson didn't go on to win the tournament – they lost to reigning champions and eventual finalists Brive in the last eight. Instead it was Bath that broke the English duck in the Heineken Cup, kicked improbably to glory by full back Jon Callard.

The side from the Rec, however, weren't given the chance to defend their crown. Before the 1998 Bordeaux final had even been played, there was doubt over whether next season's competition would go ahead. Having waited so long for such a tournament to come into being, it had been thrown into early chaos by a fallout over organisation and, as always, money. There were complaints that a tightly packed fixture list meant more injuries and fewer paying customers through the turnstiles, and there were predictably also gripes about the distribution of prize money. The English clubs that were the most vocal about their dissatisfaction called a boycott in January 1998 and it seemed they had broad support from the French. Whether the competition, which had now come to the end of its three-year sponsorship deal with Heineken, would take place at all was in serious doubt. The English clubs were sure that their absence would bring the competition to its knees; there was no question that if the French also pulled out – which seemed entirely likely – it would not take place.

'The English clubs' arguments are reasonable,' Jean-Jacques Madrias, the president of Brive, told the media when news of the potential boycott was mooted. 'In order that this competition remains a proper event, it must involve English and French clubs. Without English clubs, there is no point in having a European Cup.'

Thankfully for Ulster, Madrias did not speak for the whole of French rugby, but the participation of their sides wasn't confirmed until August, only six weeks before the first round of fixtures. Although it was far from ringing, the endorsement from the French did eventually come when the president of the Fédération Française de Rugby, Bernard Lapasset, emerged from a meeting with his clubs and confirmed they would participate – in this instance Stade Français, Bordeaux Bègles, Perpignan, Toulouse and Colomiers. European rugby could finally plan, knowing it still had its premier competition, albeit trimmed down.

The draw had already been made, whether in hope or expectation, with Ulster paired alongside the competition's first champions, Toulouse, as well as Edinburgh and Ebbw Vale. The province would, for better or worse, have the opportunity to test themselves against the best at least once more.

2
PRODIGAL SONS

The year 1998 will forever be one of the most important in the strained and bloody history of Northern Ireland.

For the preceding thirty years, Northern Ireland had garnered unwanted worldwide headlines on an almost daily basis as more than three and a half thousand people lost their lives in the Troubles. However, 1998 brought renewed hope for peace. Political talks had been ongoing for years in the background to the killings, but the election of Tony Blair as UK prime minister in 1997 brought new momentum.

An IRA ceasefire followed, allowing Sinn Féin to take part in fresh negotiations chaired by US senator George Mitchell, although the Democratic Unionist Party, led by the firebrand Reverend Ian Paisley, left in opposition to their presence. Controversy raged through the often tortuous process that involved Mitchell, Blair, US President Bill Clinton, Secretary of State Mo Mowlam and the Irish Taoiseach Bertie Ahern as well as leading local politicians. Disputes over prisoner releases, paramilitary decommissioning of weapons, police reform and the extent of the relationship to be established between north and south ensured that talks never felt far from the brink of collapse. But on 10 April 1998, the historic Belfast Agreement (also known as the Good Friday Agreement) was signed. In typically Northern Irish fashion, the two sides couldn't even agree on what to call the accord, but there was a genuine – although ultimately misplaced – belief that the sixty-one children born in Northern Ireland that day would be the first of a new generation never to be exposed to the same horrors as their parents and grandparents.

The document still needed to be passed by way of a referendum, and so heated campaigning followed: a giant YES banner was unfurled from the top of the Europa Hotel in Belfast city centre; while Paisley told supporters that the agreement was 'the greatest betrayal ever foisted by a unionist leader on the unionist people'. On 22 May 1998 the vote took place, and the Agreement was ratified by way of a 71 to 29 per cent margin. News of the brokered peace, said President Clinton, sounded 'around the world like a thunder clap'.

That same Easter, fewer than five miles from Stormont, there was less significant, but no less severe, change being instigated – and with influence from Dublin that not even the staunchest Paisleyite would have objected to. For under the instruction of new national coach, Warren Gatland, the IRFU had begun a repatriation drive to bring their front-line internationals home. Ulster had been decimated when English clubs got an early jump on professionalism and lured their star players across the Irish Sea. Among them was David Humphreys, the enigmatic out-half who, in 1992, had dramatically announced his arrival on the Ulster scene with a match-turning debut as a replacement to beat Munster. The southern province were leading 11–3 when the then twenty-one-year-old Queen's law student was sprung from the bench to replace the injured Peter Russell. With Munster well on course to beat their northern neighbours for the first time in twelve seasons, Humphreys had other ideas and belied his lack of experience by knocking over two penalties to bring his side within range before delivering a late drop goal to steal victory.

For a man who had captained Ireland Schools to the Triple Crown in 1990 (their first since 1974) – in spite of not having touched a rugby ball until his first day at Ballymena Academy in 1982 – it seemed part of a natural progression. However, those early seasons were punctuated with erratic performances. 'I'd play well some days and some days I was terrible,' he says. 'It was embarrassing some days how poor I was. Now, when there's trial by social media after every game, I would probably have been written off. Back then, I remember George Ace of the *News Letter* and Jim Stokes at the [*Belfast*] *Telegraph* being the only people at the games, and they decided whether you were any good or not.'

Humphreys' prodigious talent would only be matched by consistency later in his career, and he didn't make his first Ulster start until two years after that match-turning cameo in Thomond Park. Despite having earned four A caps, when he headed to Oxford University in 1995 to finish his law studies, he was seen as Ireland's fifth choice of out-half, behind Paul Burke, Eric Elwood, Niall Malone and Alan Magowan. A virtuoso performance in the varsity match that year, though, changed all that.

At Twickenham, in front of seventy thousand spectators, the Broughshane man scored all nineteen of his side's points and, despite Oxford losing by two to their old Cambridge rivals, Humphreys was named man of the match. While cynics suggested the standard was hardly top tier, Humphreys' performance was followed up by a return to the Ulster side and another standout showing during a 40–33 win over visiting New South Wales in front of Irish selectors. His international debut came against France in the Five Nations just ten days later.

While recent years have rendered their name a misnomer on

17

both counts, it was during this period that London Irish were at their most active in recruiting players from Ireland, north and south. As the northern hemisphere's year-long moratorium on professionalism ended in 1996, Irish sides were still only offering match fees of a couple of hundred pounds, depending on the competition, in comparison to the full-time deals on offer in England. Exiles coach, the future World Cup winner Clive Woodward, was quick to take advantage.

It was at Oxford that Humphreys first had contact with Woodward, who had taken over at Sunbury-on-Thames in 1995. He was intent on reversing the previous season's relegation from England's top flight and restoring a heritage somewhat diluted by several high-profile Irish internationals switching allegiance to their English rivals. Recruiting Conor O'Shea and Gabriel Fulcher had been the first step, and Woodward quickly made the short journey north to meet Humphreys and the other Irishmen soon to earn their varsity blue – among them the university's captain for the next season, County Down native Tyrone Howe.

'We had lunch, a whole group of us, in Oxford, and it was between the game being declared open and professionalism really kicking into gear in England,' says Humphreys. 'He [Woodward] was trying to get a lot of young Irish players – that was what he wanted for the side. He told us all that two things were going to happen: that rugby clubs in England were soon to be fully professional and that in ten years they'd be paying their players like footballers. He got one of those things right, and, unfortunately, he got one of them very, very wrong.'

Humphreys was still one year short of finishing his training as a solicitor. He had twelve months to complete at the Institute of Professional Legal Studies and, under the guidance of Ireland and Ulster legend Mike Gibson, who was a senior partner in a leading commercial law firm in Belfast, he spent his first season at Irish travelling between London and his homeland. Now edging closer to his late rather than his mid-twenties, he had still never once given any thought to turning his sporting hobby into a career, always ensuring that his studies took precedence over sport, whether the ball was round or oval.

'My dream was to play for Liverpool. In those days Kenny Dalglish was the hero. But as much as I dreamt of being a footballer, I was never good enough. I loved rugby and I loved my time at Queen's – it was probably the best time I had in my career, but it was a very different mindset to what we have now. The game was amateur then. You had to get a job, you had to work, have a normal lifestyle. It was never about finding a balance because work came first – there was never any compromise or anything like that. I was to be a solicitor. Then, all of a sudden, Clive is there and there's a chance to go pro, to go to London. It was out of the blue but no matter what you're doing you have to have an open mind and be open to whatever opportunities arise even when you least expect them. It was a very, very exciting time.'

At Irish Humphreys moved in with O'Shea, and soon enough fellow Ulsterman Mark McCall, who made the switch for the 1997–98 season, became a regular visitor. In no time at all there were thirteen Irish internationals on the books, including Jeremy Davidson, Niall Woods and Rob Henderson. For the green enclave in west London, success was swift and promotion secured but, once back in top flight, Woodward didn't stay long at Avenue Road. After a boardroom fallout he was replaced by his already full-time assistant, former Ulster and Ireland captain Willie Anderson.

It wasn't only the Exiles who boasted a proliferation of Irish stars: Keith Wood had been at Harlequins for years, Eric Miller became a Lion as a Leicester Tiger, and the elder Wallace brothers, Richard and Paul, were with Dungannon man Paddy Johns at Saracens. With Allen Clarke and Jonny Bell both at Northampton, Ulster were hit hard. In all, of the twenty-nine players named in Ireland's squad for the 1998 Five Nations, five were born in the province: McCall, Humphreys, Johns, Kieron Dawson and Clarke, and two more, Bell and Davidson, would have featured in the wooden spoon whitewash if not for injury. All seven plied their trade in England. In a departure from the 1996–97 season, and offering a clear indication that the English clubs no longer considered Irish provinces as representative sides, none of the diaspora represented Ulster in that year's Heineken Cup. Going to Ravenhill, then, was like attending a film premiere knowing that the leading men were having a better time at a different party held nearby. Star power was thin on the ground.

While his main motivation was to improve the faltering national side, Gatland – who had become national coach one game into that doomed '98 campaign – was convinced this system was unsustainable, and so the IRFU's drive to bring their stars home began in the early months of 1998.

Humphreys had no plans to move home, not with two seasons remaining on his deal. Indeed, he was to wed his girlfriend Jayne that summer and had bought a house in London, but, still planning to pursue a career as a solicitor in the years to come, it was a move that made abundant sense on a personal level. From a rugby point of view, Humphreys' and McCall's season at Sunbury hadn't been going to plan – by the end Anderson had followed Woodward out the door and had been replaced by Dick Best.

Bell and Clarke were another story, having been playing under Ian McGeechan in a successful Northampton side. Clarke, erudite and not shy to fight his corner, had moved to Northampton to study law, and had met his future wife, Kerry, while the pair were at university. A hotbed of rugby, one of the few places in the UK where it is the most prominent sport, the town and club appealed to Clarke, who had initially travelled home weekly to represent Dungannon before he finally settled as a Saint. When the IRFU tried to bring him home, offering a national contract that summer, he had been at Franklin's Gardens for eight seasons.

'With a few things going on here, the Troubles and such, I thought it was time to see other things in the world and live a different life,' he says of his original decision to leave Northern Ireland. 'For a country boy from out west, it was a big step. I really took to Northampton. There was a real Irish element to it and it was a real family club. Rugby was really popular there and I played with world-class players, English internationals, Scottish internationals, South African internationals. But I didn't see professionalism coming. I'd gone to university to study a combined honours degree as a law major. I'd got married, I was working in the social services of Northampton, using the law element, and then I told my wife I was going to go back to study to do a teaching degree. I did that while Kerry was pregnant with our first child. They were testing times.'

Little did they know that more lay ahead. For if Clarke was to answer Ulster's call to return home, it was unlikely that Kerry, their three-year-old daughter, Arianne, and their newborn baby, Alexander, could go with him. Kerry was from Northampton, so the couple decided that she should stay there to be close to her own family, while Clarke took what was technically only a sabbatical from his teaching post in England.

'It was particularly hard for my wife. I didn't see her for the first four weeks after I moved home. I left her with Alexander, who was five weeks old, and she was juggling him with a three-year-old. That was very tough. I had to get on with it. I was home to play rugby, my time to do that was short, but for Kerry … without her, none of this would have been possible.'

Knowing the offers were coming, and with the added carrot of the following year's World Cup, the Ulster contingent in England kept in regular contact with each other as they debated the pull of their native land. At one such meeting, sitting in the sunshine on the banks of the River Thames, Kieron Dawson

– who had gone straight from turning out for Bangor in the All-Ireland League to a thirty-grand-a-year contract and complimentary Rover at London Irish – wondered aloud why anyone would want to leave. And he wasn't the only player to stay put. Attempts were made to lure Paddy Johns back from Saracens – winners of the Tetley's Bitter Cup for the first time that season with Philippe Sella and Michael Lynagh among their number – but the man who was by then Ireland captain saw out the final year of his deal with the London club. Jeremy Davidson, man of the series on the victorious Lions tour of South Africa the previous summer, did decide to leave England but moved instead to play for French side Castres on a big-money deal.

Safe in the knowledge that they wouldn't be alone, Humphreys, McCall, Bell and Clarke all took the plunge – as well as pay cuts – and returned to their native province. These proud Ulstermen would wear the red hand on their chests once again. Under what would be the fourth coach in four seasons, the Ravenhill side would be unrecognisable when they next took to the European stage.

3
THE HEADMASTER

The year was 1987 and there was a sizeable lump in Harry Williams' throat. He coughed and approached the door again before pausing. He'd spent his life addressing large rooms full of watching eyes. As he would say himself, he'd been coaching rugby or teaching children since the cat was a kitten. His had been a life dedicated to attempting to capture an audience. Never wanting to be the sort of speaker who relied upon the same old clichés that saw listeners roll their eyes to the heavens, he often pored over books well into the night searching for fresh inspiration and new angles.

An understanding and respectful figure, he was the consummate man manager, even when those in question were not yet old enough to call themselves men. He'd been able to command attention in the most unruly of classrooms (he'd taught at Lisnevin, a state-run young offenders' borstal close to Newtownards in County Down that would later be used as a training facility for the Northern Ireland Prison Service), and so this audience shouldn't have presented any problems.

This, though: this felt different. This was Ulster. And not just any Ulster. This was the Ulster of Willie Anderson, David Irwin, Phillip Matthews, Keith Crossan, Trevor Ringland and, until recently, Jimmy Davidson. The best rugby team this troubled patch had ever known. Jimmy D, the former flanker who, like many of his players, had first shown his credentials at Queen's University in south Belfast, had turned them into serial winners, overcoming an indifferent first season to win three consecutive interpro titles as well as overturning Australia when the touring Wallabies pitched up at Ravenhill. Now, with Davidson gone to take the Ireland job ahead of the inaugural World Cup, it was up to Williams to pick up the baton.

It had been a smooth transition so far, with the team touring Zimbabwe and taking on Yorkshire, albeit without the cohort of Irish internationals, but standing outside the changing room door for the first time ahead of a big game – Munster in the opening round of the interprovincial championship – there was this issue of the lump in his throat. He took a deep breath and stepped over the threshold.

'I knew them from playing with the clubs, and I had a good enough relationship with them, but to walk in and be told that you're in charge of these guys, it was quite daunting. Anderson, Ringland, Davy Irwin, they weren't men who took any prisoners. It's a difficult shift from small children who would act on your every word to grown-ups who would raise an eyebrow. You have to develop a thick skin. But treating people well is important too. The amount of teaching you can do at senior rugby level is minimal, but there's the communication aspect and trying to treat people the right way. That's always the same.'

Despite his initial apprehension, and a draw with Munster ending a winning streak that dated back to 1984, things didn't work out too badly in the end. Williams' side shared the title that first year before winning it outright in his next three seasons at Ravenhill.

Originally from East Belfast, Williams had fallen in love with rugby the way so many boys in Northern Ireland do: through attending grammar school and finding a ready-made answer to being no use at football. His days in Sullivan Upper's first fifteen would be some of the most enjoyable of his life. The most memorable of all was the afternoon that a senior NIRFC side – containing a certain Jack Kyle, the Ireland and Lions hero who would soon depart for Zambia – took on the schoolboys. Not an unusual occurrence back then, though unheard of now for obvious health and safety reasons, but Williams would never forget the game in which he, like plenty of internationals before him, couldn't get near that 'damned elusive Jackie Kyle'.

Aside from forlornly chasing Ireland's first Grand Slam captain about the school pitches, Williams would look back on his schooldays with such fondness that a career as a teacher seemed an obvious choice. He trained in physical education and started work in the Bangor Grammar preparatory department before ultimately settling into Holywood Primary, a large school of almost five hundred pupils and thirty teachers in a tranquil corner of North Down.

To start, fitting Ulster around his work commitments didn't prove insurmountable. Having been coach at Bangor, where his seven-year spell had coincided with the best run in the club's history, the routine of Tuesday and Thursday nights' training and a Saturday game was sacrosanct, and in those days the provincial schedule involved only the addition of the derbies against your nearest and dearest, the odd away trip and the rare visit of a big touring side. But as the 1980s gave way to the last decade of the millennium, changes in teaching, as well as the fear that a coach's voice could become stale, prompted Williams to decide to walk away from Ravenhill.

'I always believed you shouldn't outstay your welcome. I had four good years at Ulster and I thought maybe that was time enough. There was a load of pressure in work – it was a period of great change in teaching and the time commitment of the job was getting greater. They brought in time budgets and there was a massive curriculum change. I didn't have to mark books as such, but there was a lot of time. It wasn't that you walked out the door at three o'clock. There was a lot of work at night involving curriculum planning and organising people. The buck stops with you. If anything goes wrong, it's the head's fault. It was a stressful time. I wouldn't change it for anything, but it was a stressful time. I say regularly now to pals in the game then, "How did we ever do that?"'

While Williams kept his toe in the water by working with the Ireland A side, he was back in the club game by the mid-1990s. Feeling the need to scratch a familiar itch for weekly involvement, he was made aware of a job through an old friend, Stephen Aboud. At the start of a rugby career that would eventually see him fill high-ranking roles in both Irish and Italian rugby, Aboud was then working as a development officer with Leinster Branch. Hence the only problem … the job he was suggesting for Williams was in Dublin with Bective Rangers, then in the second division of the All-Ireland League. The club was on the south side of the city, and before road development cut the journey time to Dublin to two hours, the commute was an arduous one, especially when negotiating rush hour to ensure arrival in time for training at half past seven. His late return to Holywood and then rising in time for school the next day increasingly left Williams feeling the role was untenable. By the winter of 1997, just as Ulster were completing another failed European campaign, Bective were enduring similar struggles and had lost their first four games of the campaign. Williams decided the relationship was working for neither club nor coach and he was once again out of rugby.

Still reeling from Clive Griffiths' rejection of the contract offered in the spring, and with Davy Haslett only steering the ship on a temporary basis, Ulster remained in need of a professional coach to replace Tony Russ. If a return for Williams appeared to make abundant sense, that it occurred was only down to a chance encounter. Talking to an old friend in the

Ulster Branch, Williams was told about the continued vacancy and, without giving it much thought, told his acquaintance he would be interested if Ulster were. There was a flippancy to the remark, but it soon evaporated when he found himself sitting in front of IRFU treasurer John Lyons talking numbers.

Lyons, a future president of the IRFU, had been charged with ironing out a contract long before Williams had decided whether or not he was genuinely in a position to accept one. Things were very different to when he'd last led the side: the game had gone pro, he was now fifty-five and a grandfather to boot, but the lure proved too strong.

'I don't know what made me say it,' Williams remembers of his assertion he'd consider a return. 'I hadn't thought it through. I had a month or so to think about it, and then the letter came through the door. There was no interview – they wanted to prepare a Heads of Agreement. I went with my wife and we sat down with the IRFU. Will I? Won't I? If I don't do it, I'll regret it for the rest of my days.

'I'd hoped to take a career break of three years but that wasn't fair to the school. The board of governors had been very good to me, letting me away for Ulster duties and Ireland A. I never really asked them but they never complained. I decided to make a clean break and take my chances. A former pupil of mine went through the contract, and it was sorted in a way that no matter what happened I was getting the three years.'

For the first time in his life, rugby was now work for Harry Williams. Work that was only beginning.

While Williams benefited greatly from the IRFU's efforts to bring home Ireland's international stars, he needed both a back-room team and a game plan to turn around a side that had lost seven of their nine games the previous season. With the staff at Ravenhill best described as skeletal, assembling a support group was essential, and with a recruitment drive more along the lines of 'Who can we get?', it is remarkable that the organisation struck upon such a successful blend.

Backs coach was to be Colin Wilkinson, the former full back who had made his first outing for Ulster under Jimmy Davidson in 1985 and who had continued to feature during Williams' first tenure. The Malone man was thirty-one before he debuted for Ireland, and he was made to wait even longer for his first cap. Jim Staples had been Ireland's full back since the Five Nations championship of 1991, including at the World Cup later that year. However, when the London Irish man suffered an injury on the eve of the '93 campaign, a season when the Irish national team was at a particularly low ebb, Wilkinson was given the nod for the first game against Scotland ahead of Ciaran Clarke after another candidate, Conor O'Shea, fractured his ankle in a club match for Lansdowne a week prior. Wilkinson's response to his belated selection for national duty: 'There must be a God after all.'

That match, unfortunately, was anything but divine with Ireland losing 15–3 in a contest typical of its time. When Irish coach Noel Murphy tried to claim that there were silver linings to take from the game, he was asked to name them by starting wing Simon Geoghegan. A piercing silence followed. As told in his book *From There to Here*, the *Irish Independent*'s Brendan Fanning's assignment in the aftermath was to phone the players and ask why they 'were all such wankers'.

In the post-mortem that followed, Wilkinson's physical cap was forgotten. After the IRFU realised their error, it was sent post-haste, and it would prove to be an even more prized possession than expected as he was never handed another. Clarke got the nod for the next game, and the era of O'Shea was to begin later that season.

A free runner, and even freer spirit, Wilkinson was once described by former Ulster secretary Ken Reid as 'a sportsman from another age, before it all got serious'. Working as a car salesman in 1998, the gift of the gab was a prerequisite that proved essential in rugby too. When he could get away from his day job, he was a key figure in helping to keep players, especially the kickers, loose at the most high-pressure moments. The squad also had the advantage of a team doctor – David Irwin, the former British and Irish Lion, who, in his playing days, had made his house calls still showing the scars of the previous weekend's game – with very considerable rugby expertise, especially when it came to backline play.

As for tactics, Williams was not out to reinvent the wheel. What became known among the players as 'Harry's Blue Book' was a relatively straightforward document – with Simon Mason's majestic kicking ability and the off-the-cuff artistry of David Humphreys, things didn't need to be overly complex. Pressure and territory were to be prized as if they were treasure, and Mason was relied upon to kick the resultant penalties from sideline to sideline in the opposition half. When more was required, inspiration would come from Humphreys. Hailed as the most 'technically knowledgeable' forward in his pack, Allen Clarke would be vital at the set piece.

With a largely experienced panel in his expected starting side, one that all of a sudden boasted eight players with international expertise, Williams decided that ensuring team spirit was at its peak would be his paramount concern. He believed once that was in place, performances would follow.

'I couldn't change their skill sets greatly but the idea from the outset, which I never told anybody until now, was to create a team and then people would have to fit into that. They were a great group of fellas, you couldn't have said a bad word about them in my eyes. They all got on, there were no fractious moments. There was an awful lot of mickey-taking, and that was important, but you had to be able to take it as well as give it.'

Williams would learn that the hard way: when taking the squad for a paintballing excursion to Monaghan, he found himself cornered in a bunker, being pelted by those supposedly on his team. Fun at their coach's expense didn't end there. Turning up to training after a holiday in the Spanish sun, Williams was dubbed 'Big Ron' by Andy Ward in honour of the perma-tanned former Manchester United coach Ron Atkinson. The nickname stuck.

Despite the quick-to-develop camaraderie among the squad, the initial returns weren't promising. Williams spent many early sleepless nights wondering if stepping away from his teaching career had been the right decision.

4
FAMILY TIES

During the Troubles, there often wasn't much that brought people together – but Barry McGuigan's boxing wins had a unifying effect. Born in 1961, the 'Clones Cyclone' was a figure feted by both sides of a divided community; a Catholic who married a Protestant, a Monaghan native with British citizenship, a man who had represented both Northern Ireland and Ireland before turning pro in 1981.

McGuigan went on to produce one of Ulster's most memorable sporting occasions when, in June of 1985 and boasting a 26–1 record, he was finally handed his shot at a world title. The twenty-four-year-old seized his big chance, winning a unanimous decision over Eusebio Pedroza after fifteen gruelling rounds. The Panamanian had defended his title nineteen times over a seven-year reign as the WBA featherweight king before he was bested by the wee fella from just over the border with thousands of Irishmen – George Best, Alex Higgins, Dennis Taylor, Pat Jennings and Willie John McBride among them – there to witness the feat, having made the pilgrimage to Loftus Road in west London.

In a year that would bring the acrimonious Anglo-Irish Agreement – a pact that granted the Irish government an official role in the affairs of Northern Ireland – and only ten months after the Brighton hotel bombing had seen the IRA narrowly fail to assassinate the British Prime Minister Margaret Thatcher, McGuigan's win and subsequent hero's return to both Dublin and Belfast offered a rare good-news story. As the man himself later reflected: 'The shadows ran deep. And my fights felt a little like sunshine.'

The fight was an event that stuck in the mind of a young Simon Mason, watching from his Liverpool living room, part of the twenty-million strong audience. He had familial ties to Dublin and Navan – his Irish grandmother sang along as Pat McGuigan, Barry's father, gave his rousing pre-fight rendition of the old ballad 'Danny Boy', and the big fight nights helped forge a keen appreciation of his ancestral homeland in the mind of the young sporting fanatic. Less than a decade later, he'd be right in the thick of another quintessential Ulster experience – getting soaked to the skin at a game of rugby at Ravenhill.

In November 1994, at the home of Ulster Rugby, Mason made his debut for Ireland under-twenty-ones on a side that featured a heavy hometown presence, with Jonny Bell, Kieron Dawson and Jeremy Davidson all in the line-up. It was the full back, though, who made the biggest impression in the rare win over England, kicking all his side's points in a rain-lashed 12–8 victory.

Studying surveying at Leeds Metropolitan, Mason was the coming man of Irish Rugby only a little over a year later when he was called upon to make the leap to the senior side and was handed his first cap against Wales in the Five Nations of 1996, taking the place of the concussed Jim Staples in the number fifteen jersey. Neither Ireland nor Wales had a win coming into the contest, but Ireland were by far the better side at Lansdowne Road, running in four tries with Mason adding a further ten points from the kicking tee. It was enough for him to keep his place for the following week's game, earning another start against England, the nation of his birth, in Twickenham seven days later.

'I was on the crest of a wave,' he says. 'I'd played Irish under-twenty-ones, I'd been at Newcastle and then I'd been given the chance to play for Orrell. They were a really good club just as they came into the Premiership, with guys like Austin Healy and Dan Luger. The next minute, I was into the Five Nations and starting at full back for Ireland.'

Things didn't go his way for long, however. He left Orrell for big-spending Richmond a few months after his Ireland bow, aged just twenty-two, signing up at the London club where England's Ben Clarke and Richard West, Argentina's Agustín Pichot, and the Welsh trio of Scott Quinnell, Adrian Davies and Andy Moore were all teammates. While plenty would be happy with the glamour of London and the pay cheque to match, Mason felt left out in the cold when selections didn't go his way during his second season. On the international front, matters were hardly better. Having won his third cap against Western Samoa, he seemed to be one of the men Gatland left to carry the can for the embarrassing loss. The five tries to one reverse prompted the coach to make eight changes for the next game, Ireland's most in nearly two decades, and Mason was among them. Even before the IRFU edict some eighteen months later that home-based players would be favoured in national selection, Mason hadn't been able to regain his place in an Irish side.

'It had been a great opportunity to go to Richmond, especially with the players that we signed,' he recalls. 'And there's no point denying it was a good move financially, too. I went there, we had a good season and it was like a big-spending Premier League club. But that meant more and more players coming in and the next season I was a bit-part player essentially. When you were training really hard, you wanted to play. To be honest, big money and sitting on the bench, it just didn't appeal to me. It felt like a waste of my time.

'I still felt I had unfinished business with Ireland. Beating Wales in that Five Nations when I was so young, it felt like I'd been fast-tracked into it. Then I played crap against Western Samoa and all of a sudden, I was never seen or heard of again. That wasn't how I wanted the story to end.

'I'd kept in good contact with a lot of the old Irish lads who were at London Irish. When they went back to Ulster, Humph was saying there'd be an opening there. His pitch was that I could take the goal kicks. He's always been chilled like that, he wasn't that bothered about the ego or anything or how it might look if he was a ten not kicking the goals.

'I had to take a massive cut in wages but that wasn't an issue for me. I just wanted to feel welcome again. It was important to play alongside the people who respected me and believed in me. I remembered playing that game for the under-twenty-ones and how comfortable I felt in Ravenhill. I always thought it was a great place, and it felt like it was meant to be.'

Still, despite Northern Ireland moving towards an uneasy peace, there remained a perception of life in Ulster that was impossible to avoid, even if it proved to be more worrisome to the full back's family and friends than the man himself. Mason arrived in mid-July, marching season, the time of year that often sees sectarian tensions at their highest.

In the summer of 1998 relations were proving particularly strained. The newly created Parades Commission, after three years of violent stand-offs at Drumcree, rerouted a march so it wouldn't pass through the nationalist Garvaghy Road. The stand-off that ensued saw approximately a thousand members of the Royal Ulster Constabulary, and a similar number of British soldiers, deployed to the area to deal with over two and a half thousand public-order incidents.

As Mason got off the boat, the news featured reports of one hundred and forty attacks on houses in nationalist areas. One petrol bomb attack on a house in Ballymoney tragically killed three brothers, aged 8, 10 and 12.

While his nearest and dearest worried about just where the twenty-four-year-old had chosen to play rugby, Mason remained open-minded.

'You couldn't help but see things on the news, and that had been the case for a while, I suppose, but I was quite excited about living somewhere like Belfast,' he remembers. 'Living in London, I knew what it was like to be judged on where you were from. My mum used to go mad at people saying I was a Scouse because I was from the Wirral, but down there I heard it all, I had all the "Scouser" stereotypes thrown at me. It's the same mentality with Northern Ireland. I knew the reputation wasn't fair and I thought the people in Belfast were a lot like in Liverpool – that's what I wanted after Richmond.

'I was a lad from Liverpool called Mason, so I couldn't have hid the fact I was a Catholic, but it wasn't something that made me think, "Wow, this is a big thing." I just felt it was an opportunity. I wanted to play somewhere you felt part of a community, not like London where Richmond could be playing Harlequins that afternoon and you'd get the feeling that nobody was any the wiser. It had a bad rap, but as soon as I arrived I thought, "Yeah, these are my people."'

Assigned to Ballymena, the club of Willie John McBride, Syd Millar and a host of his new Ulster teammates, Mason spent his early days in Northern Ireland living with Pat and Rodney Cole in the town some thirty miles north of Belfast. Mason had let the Coles know when he would be arriving. It turned out they wouldn't be at home – but the fact that they were happy to leave a key under the mat immediately showed how different Ballymena was to London. The trusting nature of his hosts and the warm welcomes he received everywhere he went made him feel more at home than he ever had in vast, anonymous London.

On his first days at Ravenhill Mason left Ballymena for the stadium as the Coles left for work, giving him enough time to change and be out on the field practising his kicking as the other players arrived. The teacher's-pet wind-ups began in no time at all and, almost immediately, he felt part of a team once again.

The other English accent to be heard in a changing room now swollen with professional players was the jovial booming of Justin Fitzpatrick. Born in Sussex to Irish parents, he had been on the books of London Irish since he was sixteen years old and had been called into the Irish squad for the tour of South Africa in the summer of 1998. His former London Irish colleagues Mark McCall and David Humphreys needed little encouragement to talk up the benefits of their native province. 'I'd been really impressed with Justin that year I'd been at Irish,' recalls McCall. 'It just seemed he'd be a good fit, and I knew it [the front row] was an area that Ulster would be short in as well.'

Already on the lookout for a new challenge, Fitzpatrick was all the more tempted by the Ulster approach given his desire to further his burgeoning Ireland career – which began in South Africa when he took the starting spot of injured Reggie Corrigan.

Fitzpatrick signed with little hesitation and teamed up with Willie Anderson, his old London Irish boss, at Dungannon, a side that then sat in the second division of the All-Ireland League and that suddenly boasted a line-up that included Humphreys, McCall, Allen Clarke and Jonny Bell.

All the pieces of the puzzle were now in place for Harry Williams, but finding how best to fit them together would initially prove quite the battle.

5
HUMBLE BEGINNINGS

With the continuing issues of paramilitary decommissioning and prisoner releases threatening to derail the Good Friday Agreement and the fallout from Paul Gascoigne being unceremoniously dumped from the England football squad ahead of the World Cup in France dominating public consciousness, there wasn't much room on either front or back pages as Ulster's season began in the summer of 1998. Indeed, with their big-name recruits either in South Africa with Ireland – a tour that would cause Harry Williams plenty of consternation when winger James Topping was returned home with a broken collarbone after only twenty-seven minutes of action – or, in the case of Simon Mason, yet to arrive, the large group that first assembled in early June could walk through the halls of Queen's Physical Education Centre without receiving a second glance. Still something of a ragtag bunch, they hardly looked like a rugby team ready to take on the best that Europe had to offer, not least as at that first session of the season Williams had them playing basketball.

In all, Williams had fifty-one players under consideration ranging in age from the grizzled thirty-four-year-old Rab Irwin, a prop who just three seasons prior was turning out for CIYMS's social team, all the way down to fresh-out-of-school Paddy Wallace, the out-half who teamed up with Brian O'Driscoll and Donncha O'Callaghan to help Ireland win the IRB World Youths Championship back in April and who would be attending university in Dublin come September.

In a massive increase from the season past, nineteen of the group boasted the job title of professional rugby player, for the time being putting on hold their careers as lawyers, dentists and accountants. There remained, too, a large group of players amusingly dubbed part-timers. These were the men who were still holding down full-time employment elsewhere and battling to stay in contention for their native province by bookending their working day with training sessions.

It was one such player, Andy Matchett, who Williams named as captain for his first game back in charge, in what passed for an exotic fixture against the Spanish Barbarians in San Sebastián. Matchett, who worked in sales for Clerical Medical, knew Williams well from his first days in an Ulster jersey but since then, in the words of a local journalist, he'd been 'in and out of the team like a fiddler's elbow', most recently involved in a back-and-forth battle with Dungannon's Stephen Bell for the number nine jersey.

Talk at home centred on which paramilitaries – such as Johnny Adair, the leader of the Ulster Freedom Fighters in the Shankill area of Belfast; Patrick Magee, one of the Brighton bombers; and Padraic Wilson, the former leader of the IRA in the Maze prison – would soon be freed under the Good Friday Agreement. The running joke in the Ulster camp was that in going to the Basque region, where ETA were waging its own war for independence, the Ulster Branch had arranged the only away trip they could find that would possibly be more dangerous than staying in Northern Ireland. The troubled political situations in their homelands aside, the outfits didn't have much in common.

The game was to be played in the cavernous Anoeta, the home of Real Sociedad, which could hold almost thirty thousand.

With the Northern Ireland football team beaten 4–1 by their Spanish counterparts in the same week, Ulster hoped for a better fate on their own Iberian travels, but upon arrival were met by the same oppressive heat that the footballers had faced. The welcome was just as warm, if a little unconventional, with Jan Cunningham and Andy Park doing their best to suppress their amusement when Matchett's role as captain saw him presented with a commemorative beret that, respecting convention, he donned for the prematch team photo.

With the kick-off moved by two hours so that local television could air the game, the Euskarian supporters in the stadium and watching elsewhere were treated to a big win by the home team, which boasted seven French internationals in its number, including Jean Michel Gonzalez as hooker – whose status as a regular for Les Bleus for half a decade had earned him thirty-five Test caps. Their Cameroonian-born back rower, a stack of muscle known as Serge Betsen, was still waiting for his second French cap, but nobody who felt the full force of his power that day was left with any doubt it would soon arrive.

In contrast, Ulster's collective contained plenty who had little or no experience playing for the province and others who were working their way back from serious injury. Portadown winger Neil McCluskey had suffered a string of knee problems since making his debut against Harlequins eighteen months prior but found himself back in the number eleven jersey on his return to fitness, while twenty-nine-year-old Malone out-half Michael Niblock, another who had been beset by knee troubles, was handed the reins at fly half.

Beat out of the gate in an environment described as a 'debilitating sauna', Ulster seemed out on their feet after the first quarter and trailed 21–6 at half-time with Park knocking over two penalties for their only points in the first forty minutes.

Sitting pitchside, Williams found himself transfixed by the opposition's forward play. 'We got slaughtered – they were absolutely superb,' he remembers. 'They were the first team I ever saw going around the corner from the ruck. And they didn't come around in ones or twos either, they came around like a flock of pigeons. It was incredible.'

The second half was a more even affair, with outside centre Sheldon Coulter's performance and brace of tries the highlight, but the visitors were never able to truly stem the tide and fell 57–34. For half the squad that game was their only representative action of the season. Speaking after the game Williams didn't read too much into the result. 'It's been a very useful trip. The main negative was that we lost but that's all. The game itself was able to highlight the general areas where we have to work throughout the close season and in the main, it was a youthful bunch.'

Outperformed on the pitch, it was a similar mismatch after the final whistle.

'Afterwards they wanted us to sing a song,' recalls Williams. 'It was some discordant rubbish our boys produced then they stood up and it may as well have been a choir, all singing in Basque.'

The coach was encouraged, though, by the showing of Tony McWhirter in the back row. The former Dundee dentistry student had been turning out as a lock throughout his short Ulster career, but Williams was keen to see him at the base of the scrum, adding him to a loose-forward depth chart that included Andy Ward, Stephen McKinty, Dean McCartney and Stuart Duncan. The early returns at the very least were positive.

Looking to build camaraderie among his reconstituted squad, Williams always had team building at the top of his agenda, and the players were given the opportunity to let their hair down for the rest of the trip. Keen to show their guests some of the local customs at the post-match function, the hosts had arranged for steaks to be grilled on stones, which went down well with the Ulstermen until they realised there were considerably fewer cooking surfaces than players. Faced with a potentially lengthy wait, and in the age-old tradition of the Front Row Union, Rab Irwin ate his meat raw – in fact, it may well have still had a pulse – but copious amounts of the local red wine at least made it more palatable.

When the travelling party returned from Spain, some more bleary-eyed than others, preseason really began. In those early weeks it was Harry Brennan calling the shots, the man who, in a progressive step, had been appointed the province's strength and conditioning coach in 1996. The decision was made that if Ulster weren't going to be the best team in the European Cup that season, they would certainly do their damnedest to be fittest, evidenced by notably brutal running sessions on the pitch.

When not sprinting in the rare summer sunshine, the players were dispatched to what passed for Ravenhill's gym. Built underneath the main stand, in a structure that previously housed the spectators' bar before and after games, Ulster had to beg, borrow and steal all their equipment, giving them a sufficient number of second-hand weights and mats but precious little else. One concession to modernity was a pneumatic scrum machine that sat in the corner, Williams' pride and joy throughout the preseason. The only issue came with the need to keep it indoors. As the coach, a former prop himself, jacked up the pressure hoping to see his forwards sweat, the players' focus had to stay on keeping their balance without the benefit of studs. Thankfully scrum sessions were soon permitted on the pitch thanks to the gifting of a scrum sled from Arnold Clarke, father of the side's hooker Allen.

'That's how times were,' laughs Clarke. 'We maybe didn't have the budget to go out and buy a state-of-the-art scrum sled, so we looked at dimensions, and, with my father being a classy carpenter, knocked something together. We just took a sled template and put pads on it. I remember coming back after I was done playing and it was still there, sat in the corner. Without being unkind to us, we were hardly going to smash the pads off it, so it was there for many a year until the wood rotted.'

When the end of July rolled round the squad were fully assembled and were on their travels again, this time for a six-day training camp in Loughborough. Once more, Williams looked to strike the right blend of physical exertion and team building, and it quickly became clear that he had a group more than willing to partake in both. It was training, though, that provided the trip's first real moment of mirth.

Holding tackle bags is never the most engaging activity, least of all when you're a five-foot-seven winger about to be struck by a back-row forward looking to unleash all his power into the hit. As Sheldon Coulter saw Stuart Duncan bearing down on him, he prepared to absorb the impact knowing the odds weren't stacked in his favour. If he regained his balance before being knocked to the ground, it would be considered a success, yet, somehow, as Duncan lowered his shoulder into the bag, it was his hulking frame that went tumbling; the mouthful of turf all the more unpalatable for the joyous reactions of his teammates ringing in his ears. With players doubled over in laughter, it was a wonder Williams got anything more done that session. The high jinks continued for the rest of the day, and in the evening the squad were split into groups to compose and perform a song. A pool of players were keen to immortalise the day's events using Oasis's 'Wonderwall', which had become a Britpop anthem following its release in 1995. 'Backbeat, the champ is off his feet, Shelly's gone and knocked him out', went the altered lyrics, bringing the house down long before the chorus.

The back-and-forth between Coulter and Duncan didn't end there, with Duncan, one of the squad's elder statesmen, having something of a big-brother attitude to the younger, smaller man: 'Nobody picks on him but me.' Heating a spoon in a scalding coffee cup before pressing it on the other's neck became routine practice but, when the mischievous winger played the trick one too many times, Duncan sought revenge. On a night when soup had been on the menu, Coulter conceded that this gag might have run its course when a large ladle made searing contact with his skin.

The trip culminated in the thirty-nine players being split into two teams and sent after each other hammer and tongs. Referee David Napier of Ballynahinch was flown over specially to officiate the potentially combustible encounter – perhaps his presence was the reason why one cut eye was the sum total of collateral damage, but even he was powerless to stop a player chasing another the whole way round the pitch after a perceived late tackle.

Back on Ulster soil the home crowds could hardly have been described as flocking to see the side in action when Ravenhill hosted its first game of the season, a friendly against Morocco just four days before the opening interpro of the year against Leinster in Donnybrook. The north Africans had virtually been playing rugby since the day the French Foreign Legion landed in the early twentieth century, but they didn't play their first game in the international arena until 1931 and had only become a member of the IRB in 1988, coming to Belfast ten years on as a warm-up for their ultimately doomed qualifying campaign for the 1999 World Cup. One Moroccan would make it all the way to the final of the tournament, though: Oujda native Abdelatif Benazzi's talents saw him plucked from the relative obscurity of the Atlas Lions to represent France.

Ahead of the game Williams addressed the media, stressing that returning Ulster to their previous status would be a gradual process. 'I certainly know what I want and I know that it can be achieved,' he told the assembled press corps. 'We used to be feared – to come to Ravenhill and win was a rarity. Things won't happen overnight. By chance Ulster might hit the jackpot but realistically it will take at least three years.'

The coach wasn't the only one who believed the idea of

Ulster winning silverware was still some way off. Indeed, when the players gathered for their eve-of-the-season squad picture, photographer Esler Crawford was met with glum faces. 'For goodness sake, lads, smile,' he pleaded with the players. 'Pretend you've just won the European Cup.' The thought was enough, at least, to raise a couple of wry grins. Against opposition that could hardly be considered glamorous, only hundreds gathered for the final tune-up and witnessed what can be described as a contest in name only. Ulster scored three tries in the first sixteen minutes and eventually racked up fifty points – the single blot on their copybook coming from an intercept try from Hamil Amina. The only real concerns were knocks to Andy Ward, Allen Clarke and Gary Longwell that put in doubt their participation against Leinster just ninety-six hours later. Despite the short turnaround, though, all three were passed fit and it was an unchanged side that travelled to Dublin.

With Vincent Costello at number eight for Leinster, the derby provided a real test of Tony McWhirter's fledgling back-row credentials. Meanwhile Gabriel Fulcher's return home from London Irish saw him straight back into a blue jersey and captaining the side. On the whole, though, it was a youthful Leinster panel with four debutants, among them a young Lansdowne centre, via County Meath, by the name of Shane Horgan. Though the man who was soon to become ubiquitously known as Shaggy marked his red-letter day with a crossing of the whitewash, nobody in the host's ranks could live with Andy Ward. The flanker was in imperious form and scored two tries – Williams even speculated afterwards that it might well have been the best game the Irish international had ever played. Overcoming a messy line-out, Ulster had the game in hand entering the final minutes, but with try-scoring bonuses added to the interpros for the first time ahead of the championship there was a risk that even the big win would feel like a point dropped with only three scores. With all those fitness sessions under Harry Brennan paying an immediate dividend, Stanley McDowell, picked to play in the centre despite the strong claims of Sheldon Coulter, rendered the concerns moot with a last-minute try to send Ulster home with a full haul.

Less than twenty-four hours later it seemed like the least important thing in the world.

At ten minutes past three on 15 August 1998 a group calling themselves the Real IRA, who were opposed to the Good Friday Agreement and the peace process, detonated a car bomb left in a stolen Vauxhall Cavalier on Omagh's Market Street. The courthouse was the intended target but, unable to find a parking space, the bombers left their deadly device in a busy thoroughfare heaving with summer shoppers. On the final day of the town's carnival week, conflicting warnings saw the police shepherd the public towards the bomb with the explosion killing twenty-nine people. Among the dead, in what was the single worst atrocity of the Troubles, were twelve children, two Spanish tourists and a mother pregnant with twins. Illusions of progress towards peace were shattered and the eyes of the world were once again upon Northern Ireland for all the wrong reasons. International condemnation was both swift and far-reaching.

In the week that preceded the Omagh bomb, sport hit the front pages as football fans sought updates of the injury feared to end their star winger Keith Gillespie's career, but in the days that followed there was little appetite for any such distractions as the public absorbed news of the massacre, grimly following events as the dead were buried. The sight of infant coffins was a harrowing reminder of the indiscriminate nature of such terrorist acts.

Northern Ireland's planned midweek friendly with Malta was postponed, as was Omagh RFC's Ulster League game with Collegians, but it was decided that Ulster's trip to Connacht would go ahead, albeit with a later kick-off to allow the squad to join the minute's silence planned for exactly one week after the blast. Players on both sides wore black armbands over their jerseys as a mark of respect for the dead.

If it felt the game mattered little, there was still a palpable sense of frustration as Ulster blew an 18–7 half-time lead to somehow lose 21–18. The damage came after both David Humphreys and Simon Mason saw kicks charged down and returned for tries. Williams noted dryly that rather than the planned recuperative swim the next day, he'd throw his players into Galway Bay instead. He blasted the naivety of his side but maintained they were still the best in the championship. In the aftermath of their first back-to-back defeats at the hands of the Westerners in some forty-four years, few, if any, believed him.

6
SMALLY

The first paying job Mark McCall had in rugby earned him a bottle of Coke and a bag of crisps for an afternoon's work. This was the weekly reward for him and his older brother, Paul, for chasing down wayward balls at Upritchard Park, the home of Bangor Rugby Club. In the early to mid-1970s heyday of the North Down club, seven senior teams played across the eleven acres of ground just south of the town, with the McCall lads supporting the likes of Roger Clegg, Billy McCombe and 1974 British and Irish Lion Dick Milliken. All three played for Ireland during the Five Nations of 1975, the same year the Seasiders won their first-ever Ulster Senior League title.

For all their stars in that era, one of the most important men around the club in those glory days was no longer a player. Indeed, even in his days in the club's backline he had been more adept with a bat in his hand than a ball. Father to the club's two young ball boys, Conn McCall had been born in Holywood, County Down, in 1940 and quickly showed promise as a cricketer. A right-handed batsman, he had been due to make his Ireland debut against Scotland in 1964 only to see the match rained out. It was a temporary delay, though, and he ultimately finished his first-class career with over three hundred runs to his name. The game was in his blood, where it would stay long after he last struck leather with willow, and he would go on to serve as both an international selector and Irish Cricket Union president.

Similarly, his passion for rugby endured with he and Roy Loughead, who would act as IRFU President in 1981–82, forming an ever-present double act at Upritchard Park, both driving the club forward and ensuring none of their big-name players ever got too big for their rugby boots.

'Like Stadler and Waldorf of Muppets fame, the two stood behind one of the goals, and with acerbic wit, staged a side-show,' wrote journalist Jim Stokes in his profile of the club.

Conn, a former full back in his playing days, would come to be known as 'Mr Bangor', a fitting title given his standing on committees for both the rugby and cricket club, and he would act as president for the club's centenary season, instrumental in bringing giants Cardiff RFC to North Down to mark the occasion.

With that first Senior League title brought back to Upritchard Park in 1975, Bangor went on to win four of the next eight, as well as a few Senior Cups to boot, and these glory years of Bangorian rugby were not confined to the club either. Soon enough, the local school got in on the act too. With two previous Schools' Cups to their name, Bangor Grammar's history in the province's most prestigious schoolboy competition was not to be sniffed at, but nor was it anything to rival Belfast's Big Three: Methodist College, Royal Belfast Academical Institution and Campbell College – all of whom felt that a trip to Ravenhill was a celebration to be treated like Christmas – marked, without exception, once a year. The 1985 Bangor Grammar squad, however, kick-started a run that really upset the apple cart.

Captained by Michael Webb, a future doctor and medical officer to Ulster and Irish teams, the group included Stephen McKinty, an industrious back-row forward who went on to feature heavily for Ulster Rugby in three consecutive decades, and a host of other talents who caught the eye of Ulster and Ireland Schools' selectors. Scrum half Ken Woods was an all-round sporting talent who would have football trials with Arsenal, while another, Gavin Ellis, was also a multitasker. He was, according to the side's coach Dougie Rea, the only player he had ever seen who could catch the ball in one hand while combing his hair with the other.

The undoubted star, however, was one Mark Conn McCall.

Christened Small – partly due to the need to differentiate between the two sporting siblings so frequently seen around Upritchard Park; partly, no doubt, for the irresistible rhyme – the school's number ten was an understated sort, one who harboured an obvious gift but reacted to praise as if he were allergic to fuss.

Running operations from fly half, he kicked all twelve points the day Bangor Grammar overcame Omagh Academy to secure glory on St Patrick's Day of 1985, no doubt squirming with some discomfort when it was his name that made the headlines in the next day's papers. Despite being softly spoken – surrounded by the often overflowing testosterone of a changing room his words carried an even greater resonance given the effort so often required to hear them – he proved to be both a natural leader and obvious successor to Webb as captain for the next season's trophy defence. He led the charge to successive titles – Bangor finding themselves in another final only thanks to a late McCall drop goal that beat tournament favourites Campbell College in the last four, followed by a 17–4 triumph over RBAI – to see the side become the first post-Second World War team from outside Belfast to win the title in back-to-back years.

With his son at the centre of the dual success, which came in addition to winning cricket's McCullough Cup, it was natural that Conn, such a visible figure around Bangor's sporting scene, had more than a few friends enquiring as to where his offspring planned to play rugby next season. Mark was due to study at Queen's, and his new housemates in the city were already planning on switching allegiance to the navy blue of the university side. There were fears the Ulster and Irish Schools' captain would eventually decide to do the same. In the end, father knew best.

'It's normal now for parents to go and watch their kids playing in school matches, but back then it wasn't,' says Mark. 'He'd come to every match we played: even if it was under-twelve As on a Tuesday afternoon, he'd be there. That was for our whole family ... I always wondered how his work must have felt about it. He had a real passion for sport. He wasn't pushy, but he was certainly more into that than academics. Whether we did well in school wouldn't have been important to him – he just wanted us to get stuck into sports.

'He was a better cricketer than a rugby player but it was always both – always rugby in the winter and cricket in the summer. He had a massive passion for the club in Bangor and he'd have spent a lot of his time up there. He'd coached the club, but at one time or another it felt like he'd filled just about every other role, too, so it always felt only natural that me and my brother would spend a lot of time there.

'My dad obviously wanted me to play for Bangor. They were a really good side at that point. They had been successful around those years and they had a lot of Ulster players, even though at the time that was just for the interpros and a few other games scattered over the season.

'But it was a difficult decision. I was going to Queen's, my friends were Queen's players. It was difficult to turn them down, and, on reflection, I probably shouldn't have. But at the time I was still a ten, and Ricky Cullen, he had been on the first team for a few years. He was outstanding, so they were settled in my position. I could have made a different decision but I ended up having a great time at Bangor.'

The start of the All-Ireland League came a little too late

for Bangor who, shortly after McCall left school, lost Harry Williams to Ulster. The revolution of the club game, and the establishment of an island-wide competition to involve forty-eight sides, arrived in 1990 with Bangor starting out in Division Two. Come the summer of 1997, they had sunk to the fourth tier.

McCall had by then finished his law degree and was working in the Police Ombudsman's Office, or as it was called then the Independent Commission for Police Complaints. He was twenty-eight years old and recently married when the familiar voice of Willie Anderson came on the line, asking him to join London Irish. Clive Woodward had gone but the former national captain had been continuing efforts to ensure the squad's Irish identity. With professionalism still nascent, a twelve-month deal was offered. The short-term commitment left the young couple with a tough decision to make.

'About five seconds,' says McCall remembering how long it took him to weigh up his options. He would move to Sunbury, joining the likes of David Humphreys, Jeremy Davidson and his fellow Bangor man Kieron Dawson, while his new wife Kerry, whom he had married in Mauritius shortly before, would keep her job in sales and marketing at Shell and travel back and forth as much as possible. Airport goodbyes on a Sunday evening became an unwelcome part of the weekly routine. Having missed out on the experience of university rugby, life in the Premiership with a group of like-minded souls proved to be an adequate replacement. With a healthy number of the Irish squad still only part-time, McCall and his fellow full-timers were required to do weights on their own schedule, usually in the afternoon, before an early-evening pitch session. With no alarm call first thing in the morning and left to their own devices in the evening, a cadre of the Exiles were able to keep the kind of timetable usually reserved for those worrying about end-of-term finals.

When the IRFU began making moves to bring their

internationals home, Kerry McCall had been planning to move to England so that the young couple could make the most of London life. But Warren Gatland's new stance had for the second time in twelve months given McCall serious food for thought over where he was to play rugby. On the one hand he was enjoying life as an Exile. Professional sport, especially in those early days when a blind eye was turned as to how the day was put in away from the training ground, was a world away from the Ombudsman's Office, and from Ulster, whose struggles against the likes of Wasps McCall had watched from a distance during his year away. While things may not have been going as hoped at London Irish, there was still little comparison to be made with the set-up at home. But while former Ireland coach Brian Ashton had no qualms about selecting players based in England, and indeed it was thought had wanted to move training there for the sake of convenience, Gatland made it clear that playing away from home would put players at a disadvantage for selection for national squads when calls were close.

'Import players were the exception rather than the rule then,' McCall says, 'and London Irish was almost an extension of university life – we weren't as professional as we should have been. We were finding our feet, learning how to be professional, and it really was a wonderful time in our lives. Mid-twenties, living in London, playing rugby instead of a job. It was a brilliant year but we were all given difficult decisions to make at the end of it. The IRFU were really keen to get everyone to come back.

'I was one of the older ones when the offers came in, and it was a tough choice. I loved London Irish, loved where we lived, but the IRFU made it clear that if it was close between you and somebody else based in Ireland, you wouldn't be chosen.'

While Jonny Bell was the Ulsterman abroad with the most international caps to his name – twenty-one by the spring of 1998 despite an unfortunate run of injury – McCall could rightly consider himself an Ireland regular, even if his international career hadn't always gone smoothly. In May of 1992, having been included in an Ireland tour squad for the first time, he was in a Dunedin hotel room ahead of a two Test series with the mighty All Blacks – a side they hadn't been able to beat despite trying for almost nine decades – when the team doctor rang with news of captain Philip Danaher's damaged knee ligament. It was bad news for Ireland but would surely mean a first cap for McCall. An excited long-distance phone call to Bangor followed: he was days away from joining his father as an Irish international. Until he wasn't.

At the next day's team announcement, when the players gathered to hear manager Noel Murphy reel off the names that would be starting in Carisbrook, Danaher's was the fourth read out, leaving McCall as a replacement. Surrounded by internationals, of which he was not yet one, he stared intently at the floor, trying to mask his disappointment at the news. Like his father before him, McCall would have to wait just a little longer than anticipated for his Ireland debut. In the end, the weekend still brought a Test bow as Danaher was sufficiently hobbled that he was never likely to go the distance and indeed didn't emerge for the second half of the 24–21 defeat. In such times a three-point loss was enough to count as a moral victory and, having played well, McCall kept his place for the second Test – a game more in keeping with the history of clashes between the two nations: the hosts winning 59–6.

Thanks in part to time missed with a serious throat infection and in part to the perception that, even in the days before centres were built like lock forwards, at five foot ten and under thirteen stone he was undersized for international battle, McCall wasn't back in the side until the Five Nations of 1994. He hadn't featured in the routine hammering at the hands of France in Paris but did take the place of Vince 'The Prince' Cunningham, the Dublin-born centre who had been a teammate on both Irish Schools' rugby and cricket sides, against Wales for the second round. His childhood friend had suffered a knee injury against Les Bleus and wouldn't ever get back into the green jersey. McCall suffered a rib injury on his return to the Test stage, quickly ending his own involvement. And so it went.

Two years passed before McCall was back in the fold – the 1995 World Cup in South Africa an experience that slipped through his grasp in the intervening period. But as the 1999 tournament inched closer, he was starting in Ireland's midfield more often than not and desperately wanted to be a part of the fourth global showpiece. He knew that returning to Ulster could only help his cause of being included in the twenty-six-man squad.

He was selected for Ireland's tour to South Africa in the summer of 1998, so like the rest of the returning Ireland internationals would miss the start of Ulster's preseason, but there was little doubt he would be a key driving force in the reshaped outfit. Nor was it any surprise when Harry Williams named him as the side's captain. The pair had history that dated all the way back to their days at Upritchard Park, and it was Williams who had given McCall his Ulster debut among five new caps against the English divisional champions Sunbury in 1989. The Ulster coach was a man McCall respected greatly, perhaps because both men favour a considered approach over meting out the more typical hairdryer treatment.

'The truth was he was a success,' says McCall. 'He was successful with Bangor and he was successful with Ulster previously, so he had done something right. He had a calm way about him and he was always very clear in what he wanted and what he thought was right – players like that.

'Harry had a great way of bringing the best out of people in his own quiet way. He wasn't a shouter or screamer, he just nudged people in the right direction. What he was good at as well was getting the senior players to drive his messages, that was a key strength. It was our job to focus his messages.'

Sadly, even the best-laid plans don't always come to fruition and McCall, the man so integral to the collective decision of Ulster's prodigal sons to come home, saw his return pan out dramatically differently to the way he and his coach had hoped.

When Ulster Rugby's website rebranded some fifteen years later with a comprehensive fixtures archive among the innovations, a meeting with Glasgow on 28 August 1998 was mysteriously absent. The run of games jumped straight from the trip to Connacht to the hosting of Munster, yet in between was one of the most significant matches of the 1998–99 campaign. With the hamstring injury Jonny Bell picked up in South Africa keeping him out for one more week, McCall started in the centre alongside Stanley McDowell. He got his head on the wrong side as he went to make a tackle, an occurrence that would hardly be considered rare despite his strong technique, but on impact it felt as if he had suffered whiplash. Numbness needled through his arms and he felt the power drain away down his right side. With adrenaline still coursing through his body, he put the pain to the back of his mind, somehow seeing out the game with his arms feeling like dead weights. Afterwards, though, physio John Martin immediately called for an MRI.

Under the circumstances the match result mattered little, despite providing an excellent example of what would become that season's blueprint with Tony McWhirter and Andy Matchett scoring a try apiece, while the boots of Simon Mason and David Humphreys did the rest in a 32–15 win.

In the days that followed, McCall's primary concern was whether he'd be fit to play for Dungannon the following weekend. The neurosurgeon, however, delivered a prognosis far more severe. 'There was a lack of feeling in my right side, and I couldn't lift my right arm for days. It was a bit of a worry. When I went to see the neurosurgeon at the time, I asked him if I could play this weekend and he looked at me and said, "No, you won't play again." Nowadays you would get a different decision from the doctor, but back then it was a pretty black-and-white "That's it for you."'

McCall never quite reached the stage of acceptance throughout what would be his last season as a professional rugby player and continued harbouring hopes of a playing return – on more than one occasion he was seemingly near to reclaiming his place in Williams' side. He didn't know it then but he'd never pull on the white jersey again. He had reached the end of one memorable career and was about to embark on another.

7
THE TERMINATOR

President Bill Clinton arrived in Belfast at the beginning of
September 1998 to visit Omagh and to urge the Northern
Irish people not to let the chance for peace pass, but it was
an Ulsterman in America who was of more concern to Harry
Williams. Flanker Stephen McKinty had missed the Glasgow
win due to a business trip stateside and in his absence Dean
McCartney had excelled.

The Ballymena man's return to Ulster colours from the
bench against Morocco and Leinster was his first involvement
in the provincial set-up after an absence of years. He'd made his
debut for the side in 1991, with fellow new faces Gary Longwell
and hooker Andy Adair, against the English county champions,
Cornwall. The Ballymena loose-forward trio of McCartney
alongside Irish internationals Brian Robinson and Gordon
Hamilton was one of the most impressive in the club game and
they made the step up to provincial jersey without missing a
beat. While Robinson and Hamilton went to the World Cup
in the latter half of that year, McCartney was soon pulling on a
green jersey too, turning out for Ireland's B side at Murrayfield
a few weeks before Christmas.

In the summer of 1992 McCartney headed to the University

of Pau to study for an honours degree in French and German, while also joining the local rugby club to compete in the French Rugby Union Championship. A broken leg early on in the season abruptly ended his initial campaign, when Pau reached the last sixteen but went no further. By 1994 he was back on the radar of the Irish selectors ahead of the Five Nations but, with his club employing heavy rotation game to game, the IRFU could never justify making the trip to France to see McCartney in action because they didn't know in advance whether he'd actually be taking to the field.

Upon returning to Ireland he was working as a software analyst on the Boucher Road in Belfast and was back at Ballymena, struggling to readjust to the style of play and hindered in no small part by an anterior cruciate ligament (ACL) injury that kept him out of action for ten months. By the time Harry Williams was back in the Ulster hotseat, however, McCartney was fit and firing once again, and his return to the squad a few months after his twenty-ninth birthday was a boost to the back-row stocks. When Mark McCall, whose neck injury became more worrisome only as the week wore on, was a late scratch from the side to host Munster, the coach thought McCartney was the perfect candidate to take over the captain's armband.

'As far as Dean is concerned, his display against the Scots made it impossible to leave him out and he's there on merit,' Williams said. 'We have strong competition in the back row but in any case, rugby is now a squad thing. He's a natural leader of men. He's quiet off the field but once he pulls on a jersey he's completely different.'

Nicknamed 'Terminator' in honour of his imposing physique, he was just the sort of man you'd want in your corner against a Munster side who arrived in Belfast seeking a win at Ravenhill, their first since 1979, and that had the likes of Peter Clohessy, Mick Galwey, Anthony Foley, David Wallace and the returning David Corkery in their pack. As Munster would find to their chagrin, ill-discipline was not a trait to display when playing a team that had Simon Mason lining up the shots at goal. The full back provided fifteen points off the tee thanks to four penalties and converting both his side's scores. Jan Cunningham was the first to go over, crossing as early as the third minute, while Murtagh Rea grabbed his first Ulster try following good work from Jonny Bell in the second half. Munster, meanwhile, could only muster twelve points in return and their long wait for a win in the north went on.

Rea's form was an undoubted boon to Williams in those early weeks, despite the perceived wisdom of the time being that the returning Mark Blair would earn the spot alongside Gary Longwell in the engine room. Rea was one of the part-time players in the squad, mixing rugby with his employment in the DVA's MOT centre on the Boucher Road, and had more reason than most to be amazed he was being paid anything at all to play rugby having only played his first game as a twenty-one-year-old. Living near Banbridge, he was a Gaelic footballer from his youth, a sport that holds a similar amateur ethos to the one that had previously been so entrenched in rugby.

Having shown great promise at his club, Clann na Banna, he was turning out regularly for Down under-twenty-ones and had even had one game on the senior panel against Louth. While many of the men with whom he played underage football would go on to win a pair of All-Irelands with the county in 1992 and 1994, Rea's sporting life took a different path when, in an effort to get back to match-fitness after an injury in the winter, he visited Banbridge RFC's Rifle Park for the first time. Quickly taken by the unfamiliar sport, he was getting regular run-outs for the fifth fifteens but progressing little further when a friend, similarly irked by his lack of progress at the club, moved to Dromore and encouraged Rea to join him. It was there that Rea first caught the eye of the Ulster selectors, although a serious knee injury scuppered his chances of cracking the side.

The desire to pull on the white jersey was what sold him on Malone, as the club had Ulster connections through the likes of players Denis McBride and Maurice Field, and through Cecil Watson in an administrative capacity.

After continuing his impressive ascendancy at Gibson Park, he made his Ulster debut against Scottish Saltires in 1995, with Gary Longwell alongside him in the second row, and by the early weeks of the 1998–99 season he was playing the best rugby of his life.

'I squeezed in really,' he says. 'Denis McBride and Davy Tweed were gone, Jeremy Davidson and Paddy Johns had gone across the water and they left a hole. I was lucky to get my foot in my door when I did. I was really enjoying my rugby at the time. Coming from a Gaelic background, I'd played football since I was knee-high to a duck, so it was an easy enough transition. I'd never met nicer people and everyone was so friendly. It felt like it was a mini international every time you went out to play at Ravenhill. It was a real honour to be playing for Ulster. Whenever the contracts came around, I just kept thinking to myself that this was something I'd do for nothing.'

With Rea's try having given a sizeable helping hand, the victory over Munster was an important step in Ulster readying themselves for the challenge of Europe. Despite ending the game with some badly bruised ribs, McCartney clearly relished leading the side to the win and was grinning in his post-match interview. 'I'll be all right,' he said. 'I was given the soft-shoe shuffle in no uncertain terms but it should be okay for next Friday. I don't think there's anything broken, it's just a mite sore. It's nothing to worry about, we won and that's all that matters.'

Having won four of five games, the only blip being their faltering performance in Galway, things were going as well as could be hoped for Harry Williams' second stint in charge. Top of the interprovincial table at the halfway stage, with Leinster coming to Ravenhill a week later, the northern province seemed well set to launch themselves into the first pair of European Cup fixtures with real momentum.

The best-laid plans …

Against a side they had beaten with a bonus point away from home just four weeks prior, Ulster were humbled in a game in which they lacked rhythm from the get-go and had real struggles come set-piece time. Another try from Rea and a pair of Mason penalties were all they could offer to trouble the scoreboard operator at Ravenhill, and Leinster took full advantage – Kevin Nowlan could hardly believe the hospitality, such was the ease with which he grabbed his two tries in the 35–11 win.

Ulster lost the game, but of even greater concern to Williams were the injuries. Having struggled with a chest infection the previous week, captain McCartney eventually succumbed in the fifty-fourth minute and was replaced by the returned Stephen McKinty – who came on when Ulster's race was already run, and there was a real sweat over David Humphreys' involvement in the first European clash since his return from England after he was forced from the field in the opening quarter thanks to a painful blow to his upper back.

At least nobody expected much, Williams reflected.

8
HERE WE GO AGAIN

With Edinburgh arriving in Belfast to kick-off the 1998–99 European Cup on the weekend of 18 September 1998, it felt like there was only one show in town. Unfortunately for Ulster Rugby it was a different sport in a different town two days later: the advent of another continental rugby campaign had, in the eyes of the local press anyway, been considerably dwarfed by the scheduling of Arsenal hosting Manchester United at Highbury. The Premier League pair hadn't met in a full-blooded contest since the London outfit claimed a league and cup double earlier in the year and, with such feats considered the reserve of Alex Ferguson's side for almost the entire decade, there was an eagerness to see if the empire would indeed strike back.

Despite a lack of media attention, seven thousand still turned up at Ravenhill. Edinburgh came into the game having lost six matches in a row, including one each to Ulster's interprovincial rivals Leinster and Munster, and most recently a 19–17 reverse to their own neighbours, Glasgow. Their coach Ian Rankin's preparations for their European campaign had been disrupted by injury problems in his pack: hooker Steve Brotherstone and Iain Fullarton were both out. So too – it emerged as the game neared – was flanker Carl Hogg, while international tight head

Matthew Proudfoot was passed fit to start but had been a huge doubt prior to that. Still, with fifteen full internationals at his disposal, and able to leave a pair of Lions – Craig Chalmers and Alan Tait – on the bench, Rankin was not likely to be the recipient of much sympathy from Harry Williams.

Williams sprung a surprise selection of his own by giving a first Ulster jersey to Clinton van Rensburg. The robust South African had scored twice the previous weekend in Ballymena's Ulster Senior League win over City of Derry. He was every inch the contemporary centre at twenty-three years old, six foot four, and fifteen and a half stone, even if the majority of his Currie Cup rugby for the Eastern Province had come at fly half. His move to Eaton Park had only been confirmed in late August, and he had made his debut for compatriot Andre Bester in a practice match against Hawick less than a week after arriving in Northern Ireland.

'He's what I would call a modern-day player,' Bester had said. 'He has all the skills of a fly half with regards distribution, kicking and support work. But standing six foot four and weighing nearly sixteen stone, he is a brutal tackler.'

When the signing was first mooted, Williams had quickly sourced video footage of van Rensburg in action in South Africa, and after an impressive start to life in the Ulster Senior League, he'd been invited to Ravenhill training sessions several weeks before getting the nod to face Edinburgh. His debut meant Jonny Bell could switch to outside centre with Jan Cunningham moving back to the wing. Having spent some time watching a cutting video review of the multitude of sins committed against Leinster, and plenty in the company of the scrummaging machine, the team were expecting further changes. These came, with Sheldon Coulter getting his first start of the season in place of Jonny Davis and Stephen McKinty coming in for Dean McCartney in the back row, the Ballymena man still suffering from the chest infection that had ended his game a week before.

David Humphreys had, at least, recovered from the neck injury that ended his own interpro outing, and the mercurial out-half was chosen by Williams to captain the side for a first time.

The changes made little difference.

Within seconds of the first blast of the referee's whistle, 240 seconds to be exact, his reign seemed sure to be off to the most inglorious of beginnings when Jamie Mayer and Adam Roxburgh both crossed for scores, converted for good measure and Ulster's European Cup seemed over before it began. In the days when bottlenecks out of Dublin and on to the old road to Belfast left journalists feeling as if the only way to be sure of arriving in time for a seven thirty kick-off was to leave the day before, there was some bemusement as a member of the southern press arrived late only to be told the game was up before he'd taken his seat. Hardly worth the mileage.

The same old story, thought many in attendance. A competition that had given them little, just the two wins in eight games, was set to remain true to the old script. Even against fellow projected also-rans, there was little to cheer. It was an all too familiar scene for one of the side's most experienced players, lock Gary Longwell. Having won his fiftieth cap the previous year, he had Willie Anderson's Ulster record of seventy-eight well in his sights. Now a regular, his provincial career had been something of a slow burner. While he grew up playing all sorts of sports in his Glengormley garden alongside his older brothers Alan and David, and indeed was taught by former international referee Brian Stirling in his final year of primary school, it was at Ballyclare High where rugby really took hold of the towering teen. Taller than many of his teachers by the time he started the school as an eleven-year-old, the second row provided a natural home. With his size advantage – the joke went that he never met anyone with his measurements until a school trip to Russia in fifth year, and even then it was a statue of Peter the Great in St Petersburg – the game seemed to come easy to him at first.

Having moved to Queen's University after secondary education, he impressed in an Ulster development side that took on City of Derry – having what some would still consider one of the best games of his career. The long journey with three teammates in the back of his struggling Peugeot, still bedecked with R-plates, would all seem worth it, though, when he was told soon after that he'd be travelling with the senior team on their trip to Cornwall, even if coach David McMaster prefaced the news by admitting that he didn't have any other options.

'Willie Anderson had retired the year before, Davy Tweed had been involved in quite a bad car crash and Paddy Johns had decided he wanted to be a back row that year,' Longwell remembers. 'Everyone vacated the scene and it just sort of cleared the way for me. I played with Malone's Colin Morrison in the second row, a good hardy sort. The thing I remember most about the game is getting one of the worst shoeings I'd ever had. John Martin the physio came up to me and I just told him to eff off. I didn't want anyone to know I was hurt and definitely wasn't going to be subbed off.'

A debut at the age of just nineteen did not, however, herald the start of a long and uninterrupted run in the side. The presence of Jeremy Davidson, David Tweed and Paddy Johns in those early years made sure of that. And the gentle and genial giant's attitude wasn't then conducive to the sharp end of sport either. A laid-back sort by nature, his ability and imposing physical presence weren't matched with anything like a steely determination, and evenings spent in the weights room were something of a social occasion with more time spent catching up with teammates than working up much of a sweat.

But for the man nicknamed 'Boat' – a shortened version of longboat rather than, as one former engine-room adversary turned newspaper columnist wrote, anything to do with his Roman nose – the advent of professionalism was the making of his career. With work commitments no longer an excuse, having left his position in the sales department at Kennedy Business Systems, Longwell made a vow that his conditioning would be as good as it could be.

'I didn't work hard enough and took things for granted,' he admits. 'Then Paddy Johns moved back into the second row and Jeremy Davidson emerged, and for a while I was in the wilderness. Professional rugby did wonders for me. Paddy and Jeremy went to play overseas and it allowed me to train properly and get to the fitness levels that I should have had all along.'

Transformed, he became one of the first names on Williams' team sheet, a trusted dog of war whose unseen work could be missed by the untrained eye.

'I remember reading this thing about Anthony Foley and it said that every team needs its toilet cleaners,' he once told the *Irish Times*. 'That's probably how it is with me. A team needs its street cleaners. They want me at the bottom of rucks, they want me to make the tackles, to hit rucks, they want work-rate. And I am happy to give that.'

He'd partnered Davidson in the side's first European game, the 46–6 reverse at Cardiff in 1995 – and despite having secured his starting role in time for the 1997–98 campaign, had still only won once in continental competition. Being so far behind so early in the game at the hands of Edinburgh felt nothing out of the ordinary.

'It was some gallows humour under the posts all right – or it certainly was in the group that I was with,' he remembers. 'People were just looking at each other and it was almost laughter. Laugh or cry, I suppose, in them days. It was Stephen McKinty stood beside me and he said, "There goes another European season." It felt like it was gone already and we hadn't touched the ball. It felt the same as when we played against Cardiff in that first year, that Edinburgh were going to run away with it.'

This time, though, rather than stick to the dog-eared script, Ulster tore it up.

Before they'd had a chance to develop a bead of sweat on their foreheads, they were 14–0 in arrears, but by the fourteenth minute they had taken the lead. Simon Mason showed off plenty more than just his kicking boots as he wriggled over for a fine score, while, with an Ulster penalty in between, Stephen McKinty then brushed off poor tackling for a score and to seize the advantage for the first time. With defence a seemingly optional concept, Edinburgh's Cammie Murray brought up try number five in the opening quarter of an hour to retake the lead – one of a mere seven times it would change hands on the night. Jan Cunningham crossed twice for Ulster, his second of the game coming with half an hour to go after a fine piece of misdirection from David Humphreys, and six more points from Mason had the Ulster crowd begging Gérard Borreani for the final whistle. Allen Clarke was arguing his case too, and highlighting the changing face of the newly professional game when after one decision he felt was particularly egregious the hooker turned to the assistant referee with an exasperated look and said, 'I hope you know this is our livelihood.' Amid the pleas, and in a game in which neither side could make an overwhelmingly compelling case for deserving both match points, visiting fly half Duncan Hodge dropped back into the pocket and thanks to the time afforded by a solid scrum, stroked over a drop goal from thirty-five metres out.

Unexpectedly, seventy-six points were split evenly – a share of the spoils that no doubt suited Edinburgh better than Ulster, whose campaign could still be salvaged but whose next task was a trip to fearsome Toulouse, the team that, along with Stade Français, began the year as favourites for the title. The challenge that awaited in the south of France looked all the more daunting when, later that same weekend, Ebbw Vale went to the Stade des Sept Deniers and were embarrassed to the tune of an 108–16 scoreline – a record tally for the competition and the product of sixteen tries from the hosts.

The joke around Belfast the following week was that Ulster had chartered two planes for the trip – one for the players and one for the supplies required to build a wall along their try line. To make matters worse, they would travel without Allen Clarke and Andy Ward (out with shoulder and groin injuries respectively). Against a side who had to choose which French internationals to start and which to leave on the bench, it was far from ideal. There would at least be one friendly face to welcome them on arrival: Jeremy Davidson, one of the last remaining exiles, was about an hour's drive from Castres. Having seen them up close, was there any chance Toulouse could fall foul of his native province? 'None whatsoever,' he told a travelling journalist.

Battling a migraine, Gary Longwell spent the day before the game confined to bed, and he wasn't the only one feeling under the weather as a prematch thunderstorm saw forked lightning illuminate the darkening skies and sizeable hailstones pelting the ground. Unsurprisingly it was another day best forgotten. Such travails were to be expected – indeed Ulster would not win a competitive match across the Channel for another fifteen years, but most irksome was that they were the architects of their own downfall.

Émile Ntamack had been troubling Irish defences for years. A lithe, elegant winger, born in Lyon to a Cameroonian father, he had been the first man to get his hands on the ten thousand pounds worth of silver that had been forged into the European Cup trophy when he captained Toulouse to victory in 1996. Having represented the side since he was eighteen, he was beloved by the locals bedecked in their red and black jerseys; with a reputation that preceded him wherever he played, his nickname in less politically correct times was 'la Panthère Noire'. His international career had begun in inglorious circumstances – his first two caps coming in losses to Wales and Canada, but by the time Ulster pitched up in the south of France, he'd bagged seventeen tries in twenty-seven Tests for Les Bleus, the highlight of his four scores against Ireland coming in a 1995 World Cup quarter-final.

Back after a year of injury trouble, he was not, clearly, the sort of man to whom it would be wise to give the freedom of Toulouse, but that's just what Ulster did in the game's opening minutes. His untouched canter home offered little reason to believe that any of the defensive problems from recent weeks had been rectified. But a pair of penalties by Stéphane Ougier and Yann Delaigue was all Toulouse would manage for the rest of the half. With Stephen McKinty, the previously ill Longwell and Justin Fitzpatrick all performing well, after Simon Mason struck a penalty, the visitors were more than happy with a 13–3 half-time deficit.

After the turn, however, they came undone. It started in the fifty-first minute when Dean McCartney, back in the side to cover Ward's absence, ambitiously attempted an attack deep inside his own territory but inadvertently gave the ball straight to Cédric Debrosses who had a free run across the whitewash. Ntamack's second try was another instance of poor tackling, allowing full back Ougier to escape from the Toulouse twenty-two when he should have been wrapped up in the shadow of his own posts, while his opposite wing, Michel Marfaing, had the referee, rather than lax defending, to thank for his try after it was clear on replay that Sheldon Coulter had been the first to touch the ball down. In a fitting finale, the last play of the game saw David Humphreys the next to watch his pass plucked from the air long before it reached its intended target with Pierre Bondouy intercepting and allowing substitute winger Philippe Lapoutge to get in on the act. All told, the thirty-six-point defeat was somewhat par for the course even if twenty-eight of Toulouse's tally felt decidedly avoidable.

'I think we were starry-eyed,' says Andy Matchett, who had regained the nine jersey in his continuing game of musical chairs with Stephen Bell. 'You saw Émile Ntamack and you still thought "Holy shit". It took us by surprise. You could see the head drop very early on. We still had an inferiority complex against that sort of squad.'

'That's how Irish rugby was then,' agrees Simon Mason. 'You didn't expect anything. We went on the Thursday morning and we had a few beers. It was all too much like what it was before. I think that result was what had Harry starting to worry that this wasn't going to work.'

Williams was indeed irate, not so much about the performance as at his players' perception of it. While there had been plenty of talk around the camp of just trying to avoid the same kind of humbling that had been inflicted upon Ebbw Vale, the coach who had played a part in maintaining Ulster's fearsome reputation throughout the latter half of the 1980s and beyond simply couldn't abide that such a result was being seen as some sort of quasi-victory.

'We'd looked at that Ebbw Vale game and we thought we were going to be destroyed,' says Longwell. 'There was talk at the time that we just couldn't let them get to a hundred. We played reasonably well, in the first half anyway. There were almost a few pats on the back on the way off – that feeling that at least it wasn't too bad.

'It was Harry's first hairdryer moment. He destroyed us back in the changing room. He was ranting and raving "How dare you accept that? This is Ulster Rugby, you should never be happy with that sort of a result." For a while the thinking was just "Jeez, what's his problem?" But then it sort of dawned on us that he had a point. To be happy with being mediocre simply wasn't good enough. It wasn't as if we magically turned it around from that point onwards, but it was certainly a real wake-up call.'

Williams' reaction had been so stern that there wasn't even the inclination to have a moment of mirth over one of the season's most comical events. With the replacements sitting high in the stands, when Stuart Duncan was called upon to come on in the fifty-fifth minute, he asked the stadium attendant the quickest way down to the field. Following the instructions to the letter, even if they were delivered in broken English, meant that Duncan ended up locked outside the ground when he should have been in the middle of the action. Toulouse's opinion of their opposition was so low that, had Duncan been forced to pay his way back in as a punter, it's unlikely they would have batted an eyelid. In a marquee for the post-match function, the hosts were discussing Ulster, not realising that Dean McCartney was a linguist. The flanker picked up the less-than-flattering gist.

'They're saying we don't belong on the same pitch,' he told his teammates glumly.

9
'PART-TIME' PROS

The McKinty household had never got through more loaves of bread. At six each morning, Stephen, the blindside flanker who had appeared for Ulster each season for the past decade, rose, trying not to wake his wife Joyce, and set about preparing enough sandwiches to get him through the long day. Knowing that he wouldn't be home for the better part of sixteen hours, and that he would attend an Ulster training session on either side of his full day's work as an engineer at FG Wilson, required a quantity of bread that should have led him to consider buying shares in Hovis.

With his job in Larne some twenty-five miles from Ravenhill, he would be among the first to arrive and undertake a fitness or weights session in advance of completing his nine-to-five.

'They were tough days,' he recalls. 'Leaving the house at six in the morning and not getting back until maybe half nine in the evening. It was surreal. Harry Brennan would bring us out on the pitch and the sun was barely up and you're just thinking to yourself, "Why are we here?"'

Andy Matchett, whose rival for the nine jersey was the professionally contracted Stephen Bell, had already borne witness to what was on offer in the newly professional game.

He had turned out for Bedford the year before, an ambitious Allied Dunbar Division Two side that was then financially backed by boxing promoter Frank Warren, who had made his fortune managing the careers of Prince Naseem Hamed and Joe Calzaghe among others.

Matchett played with the likes of Scott Murray and Martin Offiah at Goldington Road, and stepping off a plane at Stansted Airport and straight into a waiting, chauffeur-driven car seemed a world away from what was on offer in Belfast. He had seemed close to winning a deserved Ireland cap on numerous occasions – though his cause was hampered by the fact that he was on the disastrous development tour to New Zealand in 1997 – but was getting ever closer to his thirties at the time when contracts were being offered readily. The Portadown native, who had continued his career as an insurance executive with Clerical Medical throughout his rugby-playing days, weighed up his options before deciding to turn down a professional contract from Ulster.

Trying to find a balance between rugby and career produced a similar dilemma to that experienced by McKinty. 'The alarm clock would go at half five for me to go in and do the weights session. I remember talking to Gary Leslie and Stuarty Duncan at the time and we were all just wondering what we were doing. You were doing shuttles on the pitch as the sun was coming up and then you were going to work. You were back there in the evening and then after not too long you were starting to wonder if this is sustainable. It wasn't, obviously.'

Those whose working day was solely devoted to playing the sport had similar feelings. Rab Irwin – who the year prior had played under a part-time contract while still working as a builder – was so despondent about the early season slump that he expressed his misgivings to Chief Executive Mike Reid. He was the sort of prop who couldn't lift weights but if push came to shove could probably shift a Ford Fiesta; the 1998–99 season, during which he would turn thirty-five, would be his only campaign of fully professional rugby.

To get to Ravenhill he had taken the scenic route. The son of a blacksmith, he had played mini rugby since he was a tot and kept up the game at Wallace High in Lisburn, even though horse riding was the family sport. Indeed, his brother and sister had both won European titles in showjumping – that a teenage Irwin had failed to qualify for the championships was something of a thorn in his side. Studying engineering at Queen's, he continued to play rugby in university but found himself drifting away from the game once he graduated and took a job with FG Wilson, the same firm that employed McKinty.

'When I went to Queen's full-time, that's where I played,' he recalls. 'I'd been playing for Lisburn before, and Queen's were never going to be victorious, but every week we'd all pitch in and play. It was just what you did, it was where your friends were, the guys you played with were who you socialised with. Once I'd graduated, I'd been asked to go to a couple of Ulster training sessions, ones that the likes of Willie Anderson were running, all unpaid back then. But I was married, I was concentrating on that, concentrating on houses, cars, careers, that sort of thing. I drifted away from it. In those days, my friend was my wife and then we had our little boy.'

While working in Larne, he dabbled in the game again, playing for the local junior side before Barton McCallan, a long-time friend and former hooker who was twice capped by Ireland in 1960, convinced him to join CIYMS. After a few years in Belfast the pressure of work was beginning to tell – he'd ballooned to twenty stone, and having started out playing senior rugby was now walking from ruck to ruck on the club's social fifteen, a side that did admittedly boast former British and Irish Lion Trevor Ringland among their number on occasion. Irwin decided it was time for a change in direction, not just in his rugby but in life in general. Having moved up the chain at FG Wilson, he was nearing a promotion when instead he abruptly quit.

'I've always been willing to hop and shift,' he says. 'I'd come away with a pretty prestigious engineering degree and I had a well-paid job from a sponsoring company. I moved to FG Wilson and established a good career with them, working with 340 people in my section, but somehow I wasn't enthralled or motivated by the thought of spending any more time doing it. I'd bought a house, I was looking at the prospect of doing some property development. I'm of a personality that's happy to change, to pick things up and run with them.'

He carried the desire for transformation on to the rugby field. Having seen the crowds swarming to Ballymena in the top tier of the thriving All-Ireland League, his interest was piqued and McCallan, himself a former Ballymena man, was soon facilitating another move, setting up a meeting with none other than legendary British and Irish Lion captain Willie John McBride in order to seal the deal. Once in Ballymena, Irwin endured a baptism of fire at All-Ireland League level. An early tussle with Irish international loose head Nick Popplewell at Greystones proved a particularly harrowing scrum experience.

'I couldn't move him up or down or left or right in the scrum,' he says laughing. 'I tried all of them. I was there grunting with the effort and he was just there chuckling.'

Soon enough, though, a slimmed-down version of Irwin was fulfilling his potential at Eaton Park under the influence of his new coach, the former Springbok captain and coach Nelie Smith, who revolutionised his approach to fitness.

'Nelie had a wealth of knowledge that we were able to tap into,' says Irwin. 'He upped the training from two nights to three, which was unheard of. Mondays, Tuesdays and Thursdays, and then a game at the weekend that could have entailed leaving on a Friday afternoon and getting back on a Sunday evening. It was time-consuming but it was phenomenal – it was like a mini tour every other week. We didn't win the league but we learnt so much in terms of tactics from Nelie that just hadn't been available to anyone in Ulster before.'

By this stage Irwin had separated from his wife and was living in a rundown house that Gary Longwell had purchased with a view to moving into property development. Working in the construction trade, Irwin would drive his decades-old Land Rover to Longwell's house three evenings a week where the lock's mum would provide a cup of tea before the pair travelled the rest of the way to training with Ballymena together. In August 1997 Irwin made his Ulster debut, sprinting on to the field when Gary Leslie walked over to the sideline for a touch of treatment. Whether Leslie actually intended to come off the pitch remains a point of some conjecture, but once Irwin was on there he certainly wasn't for departing again.

The idea of being paid to play rugby, even in a part-time capacity, and three free post-training dinners a week was an arrangement not to be sniffed at, but coming into the 1998–99 season Irwin, now on a professional contract, expected a more professional approach. While the extra money was no doubt a boon, on the field he was frustrated by how little had changed in the supposedly overhauled set-up, especially given that come the start of October he had yet to start a game (stuck as he was behind Leslie). It was not long before he aired his misgivings.

'It was fairly early on and I remember being out for a run with Justin Fitzpatrick and both of us just saying "This isn't working". It wasn't setting us up to win games – something had to give.'

Frustrations boiled over into training, and during one line-out practice Irwin and Malone loose head Richard Mackey started throwing haymakers. To call it a scuffle would be a misnomer as both hardy props seemed content to let the other take his turn in throwing digs. With the shuddering thuds echoing throughout Ravenhill, and neither man seemingly inclined to hit the dirt, the back and forth could have gone on until sun up if there hadn't been more work to be done on the set piece.

For someone like Allen Clarke, an international-quality player who had arrived home with ideas of driving standards, it was an undoubtedly tough time made harder still because his young family were back in England. At Northampton, under the watchful eye of Ian McGeechan, he had witnessed the benefits of devoted preparation first-hand, even in the years before money was a factor.

'Northampton was professional in terms of culture and training long before the money came in,' he remembers. 'As far back as 1993, we were doing double training sessions in the morning and the evening and working during the day. You were coming home at night and just crashing. Geech ran a really good programme and that put you in a good position to come home and add some value in terms of what was really the first year of pro rugby in Ulster, but we were trying to cater for all needs.

'You have to recognise that in professional sport nothing else matters. You sacrifice a lot – the rewards and the experiences are huge, but you have to sacrifice a lot, that goes for any top-end sport, be it amateur or professional. One of those sacrifices was what was the best for the group rather than what was best for the individual. We were being paid to be professional but hanging about all day to train. That's fatiguing. It's demotivating.

'That will to be part of something bigger that became so evident later on in the season was lacking then. Things had tapered away. There had been a real buzz going into that first Leinster game and preseason was exceptionally good. But then the kids go back to school, people have other demands on their time and we were almost a split camp. It was like All-Ireland club rugby, coming together at night, although arguably they would have been in a better place because at least everyone would have known everyone.'

Ultimately, the catalyst for change was provided by the interprovincial trip to Musgrave Park in Cork. The common perception remains that Ulster's hopes of recapturing the interpro crown they hadn't won outright since 1993 went up in smoke when they were hockeyed by Munster, beaten out of the gate by their southern rival's increased intensity and fervour. But the 31–9 result alone fails to tell the full story. While the visitors quickly fell into an 11–0 hole after an early John Lacey try was sandwiched between two penalties from centre Mike Lynch, six points from the boot of Simon Mason and a fine drop goal from David Humphreys had Ulster with momentum and only two points in arrears at half-time.

After the turn, though, they were run ragged. Fatigued and fading, five hours from home and at the end of yet another week of fourteen-hour days, the wheels came off and there was forty minutes of one-way traffic. Munster's flankers Eddie Halvey and Alan Quinlan terrorised Ulster in a half during which they had to worry little about negating the opposition's play with ball in hand, for in truth there wasn't any. Anthony Horgan was given all the space in the world to touch down in the corner after fifty-four minutes, while substitute scrum half Peter Stringer darted through to set up a try for Anthony Foley. With time running out, and Ulster simply looking to get out of the rain, the late rolling maul that saw Mick Galwey rumble over felt inevitable. The net result was five match points for Munster and a chance to regain the title they had lost to Leinster one year before. Ulster faced a long and painful journey back to Belfast.

With only one point from two European games, and now needing to beat Connacht in the concluding interpro to be sure of qualification for next season's tournament, Harry Williams knew the campaign was teetering on the brink.

'After that Munster game, it was despair,' he says. 'We just got destroyed. I went into the changing room and the boys' heads were down round their ankles somewhere. I remember asking, "Is anyone here tired?" and all the hands went up – they were knackered. The programme we had in place just wasn't right for them. Training in the morning, off in the afternoon, coming back in at night, it wasn't working.'

From that day forward, the part-timers trained around the pros, not the other way around. No more shuttle runs as the cock crowed, or pitch sessions long after the sun went down. Instead training was held mid-morning and mid-afternoon, with one evening session a week to keep the likes of McKinty, Leslie and Matchett a part of things.

For McKinty, the player who potentially had the most to lose should those still working the nine-to-five grind be cut adrift, the decision was a welcome one.

'The overall dynamic was really positive,' he says. 'I never sensed that there was any negativity between the guys, there wasn't a split or anything. The season before, there'd only been a few professionals. I was never sure how they put their day in really – golf and PlayStation I always suspected – but the guys coming back from England were used to a more professional routine and environment. They made a big difference. It really had changed significantly and it was good to have those people to show the way.

'When we were training in the mornings and the nights, they [the coaching staff] were trying to keep the team together, I suppose, and make sure the fitness was there, but it was a difficult dynamic for the full-time guys too. They weren't there in the early mornings but the fact that they were hanging around all day waiting to train at night was probably a little alien to a lot of them by then. I remember having a wry smile because the feedback coming in was that the full-time guys were tired from the evening training. I was thinking, TIRED? We were the ones up at six every morning.

'I remember being sort of glad when the decision was made. I didn't sense it would be more difficult for me. It was maybe different because it was me and Stuart Duncan vying for the position who were in the same boat. Andy had Stephen Bell breathing down his neck so that was more difficult, but Harry was looking out for the overall welfare of the team, the dynamic and progress of the team.'

The overdue change came in as the province readied themselves to travel to Ebbw Vale in the third-round European Cup pool fixtures. McKinty, Matchett, Gary Leslie, Dean McCartney and Murtagh Rea all started at least one of the first two European games while still holding down their full-time jobs, but there was little doubt that Ulster Rugby would never be the same again. The new professional approach was here to stay.

10
THE FORGOTTEN MAN

Back in his native province, it wasn't long before Mark Blair started hearing the whispers. Although he'd been in consideration for a Scotland call-up in the months before, when he arrived home in the summer of 1998 he was the sole recruit to return without an international cap to his name and the only local player who was signed up without having previously pulled on the white jersey.

A native of Armagh, he had grown up spending Saturdays at the Palace Grounds, home of the local rugby club. With rugby having been the centre of his universe at the Royal School Armagh, he required a year in technical college to get his A levels up to scratch for the engineering degree he wished to study at Heriot-Watt. During the wait to start his university career, he was regularly turning out for Armagh's senior side, an experience that would lead him down a divergent path when he eventually made it to Scotland.

'Playing for Armagh then was a real eye-opener for me, just a kid out of school,' he remembers. 'In those days, it was probably coming to the end of the great times in the club game, but it definitely made me more appreciative of what was required – I had to work a lot harder than I had playing school rugby. When I got the grades and was off to Heriot-Watt, I went along to the freshers' week rugby trial but lasted about fifteen minutes. I had some fourth-year student trying to tell me about rugby when I'd been back home playing against some really great club sides. I figured then that it wasn't the place for me, but my parents had been across to me to help me settle and someone had mentioned Currie Rugby Club to them. They were a sort of country club, on the outskirts of Edinburgh, but only a mile or so from the university. I played two games for their seconds, got on to the firsts and played there for the next seven years.'

When Scotland began tentatively dipping its toe in professional waters, Blair wasn't one of the thirty or so contracted players split between four district sides, but that was set to change when he started turning out for Edinburgh in the 1997–98 campaign. When the SRU merged their sides to cut their now substantial wage bill, Blair still had an offer on the table, but he had also been told by his agent of interest from Ulster too.

While the likes of David Humphreys, Mark McCall and Jonny Bell felt as if they were coming home when they were in negotiations for Ravenhill returns, it was different for Blair, who undoubtedly had more friends in the Scottish rugby scene than he did back home – although he knew Simon Mason and Justin Fitzpatrick through the Exiles system. He'd put down roots across the water; his girlfriend, who would become his wife, was an Edinburgh native; and the decision about his playing future was one that weighed heavily on his mind. In the end it came down to finances. When team manager John Kinnear informed him of the substantially larger wage on offer in Belfast, Blair went to the Scottish officials and told them he would stay put if they matched the offer or at least split the difference.

'They wouldn't and that was that,' he says. 'Cheerio, I was off back home.'

As Ulster's first band of professionals had discovered, there wasn't much for a rugby player to do between the season drawing to a close and the start of the summer holidays, so the Edinburgh squad saw in the time with a few games of five-a-side.

'Not a good idea for rugby players,' says Blair ruefully.

It was in one such kickabout that he damaged his ankle ligaments, putting him out of action for the entire summer; a situation not improved by his overindulgence on a Spanish holiday. When he turned up to his first Ulster preseason, he hadn't been active for months. It didn't escape the attention of his new teammates.

'I wasn't in the greatest shape and I just wasn't well received,' he says. 'I was a stone overweight; Ulster would say two stone. I'd been asked to come back, supposedly brought over to add value, and I turned up looking more like a front row than a second row. Of course, when that happens people can disassociate themselves from you. The feedback was along the lines of "Who's this fat bloke we've signed?"

'I came back and I didn't have the same profile as Humph, Mark McCall or Jonny Bell. They were internationals and I was just another signing. I didn't have the same kudos and I understood that, but I was a bit fed up with a few guys. I'd heard from a few others about the whispers around me being fat. They certainly weren't nasty by any means, but I did feel sidelined. Whenever we were away on trips in those early months, I felt on the outside of it rather than the inner circle, and then when I started to get over the injury I couldn't get my place in the team.'

That he was outside Harry Williams' plans was made clear to him in no uncertain terms when the coach called him into his office one afternoon between training sessions. Written on a sheet of paper was the team Williams had had in his head when the season began. In the second-row positions, he'd pencilled in the names G Longwell and M Blair.

'He just turned his pencil upside down and rubbed my name out,' remembers Blair. 'He looked me in the eye and said, "When I brought you back here, I pencilled you straight in." Then he rubbed me out. I'd been in an extended Scotland squad, had been getting a regular game for Edinburgh and there I was … literally rubbed out.'

To be deemed not good enough to start was the source of some embarrassment, especially when Ulster played both Scottish sides in the early months. Given that he was not included on the bench against Edinburgh in the pool opener, some former teammates were not shy in pointing out that Blair would have been better staying put. Having been so close to an international call for Scotland, now he couldn't get near a white jersey never mind a green one.

In truth this was down in no small part to Murtagh Rea's form. When the Malone stalwart had made his Ulster debut in 1995, he was alongside Gary Longwell in the second row. That same pair had been Williams' choice for the first eight games of the season, with the hard-working Rea scoring his first two Ulster tries in consecutive weeks. While Blair had travelled to Toulouse, he watched the entire game from the replacements' bench, and saw no action again in the humbling loss to Munster in Cork.

Rea, though, was one of the part-timers, and Williams' switch to daytime training in the week leading up to the trip to Ebbw Vale meant more than a change of schedule. When the team was revealed, Stephen McKinty was the only player named to start who didn't have rugby as his full-time profession. Blair replaced Rea, Rab Irwin took the number three jersey from Gary Leslie and it was Stephen Bell rather than Andy Matchett at scrum half.

Having endured more than a few indignities since his return, Blair's confidence was brittle but he took to the field determined to show his true worth. 'It spurred me on,' he says. 'It could have gone one of two ways. I could have thrown the towel in or dug in and proved them wrong. It was important to me, not even for Harry Williams but for the other players. I knew that I needed to deliver.'

Just as Williams had always intended, Blair was playing

alongside Gary Longwell, starting a second-row partnership that had more than a touch of yin and yang. While Longwell worked himself up to high doh before a game, Blair was often found chatting about anything but rugby with the likes of Jonny Bell or Andy Park until moments before kick-off. Rooming together for the first time, the industrious and dogged Longwell told his second-row partner that he would be happy to go the whole game without touching the ball. Blair's response perfectly summed up the difference between the pair.

'Gary,' he said. 'If I had to go the entire game without touching the ball, I'd retire tomorrow.'

Having conceded 149 points in their first two pool games, the lion's share coming in the drubbing against Toulouse, Ebbw Vale welcomed Ulster with no genuine aspirations towards a quarter-final place. Already known to be no great shakes, but having finished fourth in Wales the season before, Ebbw Vale had had their confidence somewhat restored after beating league leaders Pontypridd in a 24–23 nail-biter one week prior. There was to be no such tension upon their resumption of European action, however; not with Ulster running in seven tries and Simon Mason nothing short of automatic off the tee.

Before each game, Stuart Duncan would walk up to the full back and tell him that he wouldn't miss a kick that day, and on this occasion at Eugene Cross Park the reserve flanker proved especially prescient. With the Liverpudlian's parents Des and Jean in attendance, fast becoming Ulster's biggest fans, their son went a remarkable eleven from eleven with the boot for a personal haul of twenty-six points.

Not burdened with kicking duties, David Humphreys, too, was in inspired form, producing the kind of game that gave his teammates the confidence that this was a team far better than results over the last month suggested.

'Unless you played with Humph you didn't appreciate how good a player he was, the acumen he had,' says Tony McWhirter.

'He was the best player I ever played with, up there with Jeremy Davidson and Paul O'Connell. He came across as being not cold, but very much his own man. If he didn't want to talk to you at that very minute, he'd tell you, that sort of thing. But the thinking he did on the game coupled with that raw ability was unreal. You talk about guys that are gifted, and you're talking about being able to see space and then execute too. It's different being able to see something and try it, but he could see things, try them, pull them off and still have time afterwards because he already knew what he wanted to do next.'

Growing into the captaincy with each game, Humphreys scored two tries in a 61–28 win that saw Ulster move level on points with Edinburgh in the pool. The out-half certainly sounded like he sensed the new training schedule and line-up had the potential to turn things around. 'We buckled down after the Munster defeat,' he told the modest numbers of assembled press. 'We changed to daytime training and worked hard. The change in routine certainly helped us to focus on our game – we had a lot more energy and everybody had a big lift going over to Wales.'

Playing behind a pack that remained in situ for many European games to come, Humphreys reserved plenty of praise for a new-look unit that from one to eight now read Fitzpatrick, Clarke, Irwin, Longwell, Blair, McKinty, Ward, McWhirter.

'Over the last few weeks we haven't been going well because of the silly errors and lack of ball retention. The forwards were not playing particularly well but against Ebbw Vale they were superb. They managed to keep possession through a number of phases which in turn produced pressure that brought some great tries. An out-half is totally dependent on a pack to make things happen and I had a lot of space and plenty of time. It's a long time since I scored two tries and it was good to get them. I suppose I got a little carried away in dancing in for the second but it was a little release of tension.'

Williams, too, was quick to note the contribution of the men upfront. Afterwards he sat with Blair, not long after he'd erased his name from the prospective team sheet, and told him that he'd been the best player on the pitch.

'It was the first real acknowledgement that he hadn't signed a lemon,' says Blair. 'I've so many memories of that season but that moment was probably the one that gave me the greatest satisfaction.'

Just prior to kick-off, having forgotten his own raincoat when packing for the trip, Mark McCall had borrowed the somewhat tattered windbreaker of his old Bangor schoolmate Stephen McKinty. With plenty of superstitious players among their squad, it was soon agreed that McCall would have to wear the garment to games until Ulster's next loss. His wife, Kerry, it was fair to say, was less enthused by the decision.

11
A FIRST SHOCK

The October weekend that Toulouse arrived in Belfast was already a momentous one for Northern Ireland. At a time when there was increasing concern that the institutions of the Good Friday Agreement would be destabilised by the slow progress of paramilitary decommissioning, the peace process was handed a considerable fillip when it was announced that two key political figures, John Hume and David Trimble, were to be awarded the Nobel Peace Prize.

There was hope that the high-profile recognition would give some much-needed impetus to the process at a critical juncture, something that, despite the win in Ebbw Vale, remained lacking in Ulster's European campaign. Still somewhat behind the eight ball after dropping a point at home in the opener against Edinburgh, Ulster could hardly afford for another side to take points away from Ravenhill, but few held out much hope that Toulouse would do anything other than effectively end their host's quarter-final hopes for another year.

Three weeks after their 39–3 win on their home patch, Toulouse coach Guy Novès made five changes to his side, leaving Émile Ntamack, Franck Tournaire and Fabien Pelous on the bench – but expected his altered side to maintain the same level.

'While I'm very conscious that playing in Ireland is going to be very tough, I think we have almost qualified for the knockout stages, so I reckon we will use mostly the players who have not yet qualified,' he said upon arrival in Belfast. 'But our job is to win and win well. Our team is in good shape at the moment and we don't have too many injured. We have a lot of experienced players who will be looking forward to the game. When you bring in an international player he will want to prove himself, so I'm confident we will put in a good performance.'

With terrace tickets going for only six pounds a pop, and one of the biggest names of European rugby in town, the game was unsurprisingly Ulster's biggest crowd for seasons, with early-arriving supporters welcomed by a few new additions to the stadium such as stalls selling French cuisine, a temporary team shop and face painters. There were some prematch pyrotechnics too, but once the game began it was Ulster, surprisingly, providing the fireworks.

Four penalties from Mason in the opening eleven minutes got the side into an early lead, and the full back's inspiration was not just from the kicking tee after he shimmied over for a fine score too. Michel Marfaing and captain Jérôme Cazalbou responded for the visitors but it was a raucous Ravenhill that cheered the team off into the sheds with a 17–14 lead.

Cazalbou's second try of the game, just five minutes after the restart, saw him peel off the back of a line-out to give his side their first lead of the evening, but it would prove to be short-lived. When the dust settled after a turf-churning rolling maul, it was a smiling Stephen McKinty who popped up with the ball. Ulster provided some padding to their advantage when Stephen Bell – now firmly on the radar of Ireland coach Warren Gatland – opportunistically snaffled the ball when it squirmed out of a Toulouse scrum and unleashed the muscular figure of Clinton van Rensburg to barrel across the whitewash for what would be his only Ulster try. He could have stayed at Ulster for years without getting one that carried greater significance.

Mason's conversion made it a two-score game and, even though substitute Christophe Deylaud's penalty ensured it would be an energy-sapping, nerve-shredding five minutes of injury time, the Ulstermen improbably held on. Just Toulouse's third-ever defeat in the competition, not to mention Ulster's first win over French opposition, and the buoyant crowd refused to leave until their heroes re-emerged for a curtain call. It was an event that made quite the impact on Justin Fitzpatrick; his first experience of one of Ravenhill's big nights since his summer switch from England.

'I've never experienced anything like the Toulouse game,' he gushed afterwards. 'When London Irish were struggling we had some great crowds at Sunbury, but nothing, absolutely nothing, could compare to that noise and atmosphere.'

Despite the surprise defeat for Toulouse, and something of a scuffle at the final whistle that saw Mark McCall's lucky raincoat bear the brunt of things, the French attitude towards their opponents remained friendly, and a group of players from each side, led by Stuart Duncan and Yannick Bru, whiled away the early hours over a few beers in a late-opening Chinese restaurant. When Toulouse next came to Belfast matters wouldn't be quite so convivial.

12

A LION, A TIGER ... AN ULSTERMAN?

While there weren't many other matches in contention, it was definitely the case that the victory over Toulouse was Ulster's greatest in European competition. Harry Williams was afforded little time for celebration. Instead, the coach spent the weekend feeling somewhat isolated, a long forty-eight hours of soul-searching required as he pondered his team selection for the coming Friday's game against Connacht at Ravenhill.

As Ulster's players were recovering from their exertions against Toulouse, Eric Miller was scoring twice on debut for Terenure against Dublin University. It was his first game back on Irish shores since leaving Leicester following a bust-up with Dean Richards, the man he had once battled for the number eight jersey at Welford Road before long-serving English international Richards was appointed coach the previous summer.

A Dublin native, Miller had been a Tiger since 1996, his first year in the English Midlands proving to be something of a breakout campaign. Part of a star-studded squad that included the likes of Will Greenwood, Martin Johnson and Neil Back, he had come off the bench in that season's Heineken Cup final defeat to Brive, as well as winning his first four Ireland caps. Still just twenty-one at the time, he was the archetypal bolter on the British and Irish Lions tour to South Africa in the summer of 1997 when, as the youngest member of the party, he put injuries and illness to one side to appear off the bench in the second Test only moments after Jeremy Guscott knocked over the famous drop goal that would clinch the series.

In the next fourteen months he appeared to lose form and confidence, and, crucially, he lost his Ireland place almost simultaneously. With the World Cup a year away, his return to Irish Rugby was intended as a catalyst for a return to form for the tournament. Leicester required a twenty-five thousand pound fee for his release from the last two years of his contract so there was little chance of him arriving at a northern club, but after he agreed a move to Lakelands Park over his former side Old Wesley, 'Nure President Michael Jordan joked that if Newcastle United could pay fifteen million for Alan Shearer, then twenty-five thousand for a Lion of Miller's quality was a snip.

But while he'd be back playing club rugby in Leinster, he and the IRFU informed Ulster that the wish was for Miller to play provincial rugby at Ravenhill, even though there was no guarantee the deal would be for any longer than the concluding round of the interprovincial championship. This posed something of a problem for Williams who already had a number eight: Tony McWhirter.

A year older than Miller, but without the Irish and Lions honours to match, McWhirter had been in fine form since Williams took the decision to return him to the back row for the game against the Spanish Barbarians in June. The 1998–99 campaign was the Ballymoney man's first in full-time professional rugby after his early years in the Ulster set-up had been spent striking a difficult balance between the sport and his studies. The first rugby jerseys he'd ever worn were those of a club side in

Taranaki, where his dad had played, when the recently married McWhirters spent a few years in New Zealand on a two-year career exchange. Indeed, they likely would have stayed in the southern hemisphere had it not been for an ailing parent, and so it was back to Northern Ireland where Tony was born.

With aspirations to be a dentist, he had rushed to Dundee University for his interview the day before his unfancied Dalriada side overcame the Bangor Grammar team of Kieron Dawson and Jan Cunningham in a Schools' Cup semi-final. While they would ultimately lose to Campbell College in the final, the hard-carrying number eight had done enough to impress the Ulster selectors who kept him in mind throughout his studies.

'At that stage, I just fancied going away and the grades to stay at home were higher than what you needed to go away. I could have gone professional in my third year of the course, but I talked it over with my dad – the intention had always been to get my qualifications first.

'I would have gone to class on Monday, drove to Glasgow airport on Tuesday and flew home for Tuesday training. You'd sleep on someone's floor, get up at six to get the first flight out and then back into class at ten on Wednesday morning. It'd be the same thing on Thursday, going home for training, and then with Ulster you'd either travel away on the Friday night or be playing at home on the Saturday afternoon, back to Dundee on Sunday and do it all over again. It was pretty full on but I wouldn't change it at all. There was a little bit of money but you were part-time and got your match fee. I was able to leave university debt free and had a bit of money left over for a car. I played a bit for Dundee High School FP too and it really was the ideal world. It was like now in the sense that if you didn't perform, you got dropped, you'd lose your place – but you still had a life outside of rugby, you didn't have to go looking for one, because it was just what you did. None of us had grown up thinking of being rugby players.'

In his penultimate year of study, McWhirter went through this routine only to find himself seeing no action on the pitch, sitting on the bench for months at a time, until head coach Tony Russ took him aside and told him that it no longer made financial sense to fly him back for the games.

McWhirter was reestablished in the Ulster side by 1996, but the next time an Ulster coach asked him for a private word it was to discuss Eric Miller. While Miller was not eligible for the European Cup, having been playing for Leicester well beyond the registration deadline, Ulster's next action after Toulouse was the interpro with Connacht at Ravenhill. This game, in conjunction with Leinster's hosting of Munster in Donnybrook, would decide not only which province had earned the right to call themselves the pride of Ireland, but also which three would be the representatives in next season's European competition. While Ulster were the only one of the four with no aspirations for the title thanks to their back-to-back losses to Leinster and Munster, with the uncertainty surrounding the format of next season's European Cup, it was believed a top-two finish would be imperative for qualification. Ahead of this crucial contest, and one day after Miller had trained with his new teammates for the very first time, Williams had to bite the bullet and tell McWhirter that, through no fault of his own, he'd lost his place in the starting side. At first, the news went down like a lead balloon. McWhirter thought briefly of walking away before his initial anger subsided and was replaced by a determination that he wouldn't give up his jersey without a fight.

'Harry took me to one side and told me he'd no option,' he remembers. 'I just said to him "At the end of the day, will you have to pick him just because he's here?" He said he wouldn't and that was all I could ask for. If it came down to form, and I was playing well, I had to make myself undroppable. He'd certainly be a better impact player than I'd have been off the bench – I was more suited to doing the hard stuff for sixty minutes and breaking teams down slowly.

'It was a difficult time but what could you do? You could either get in your car and sulk about it forever or you could roll your sleeves up and get to it when you got back in. I'd like to think anybody that knew me could have guessed what option I was going to take. I might have initially thrown a bit of a wobbler but I was always going to come back and try to prove my worth.'

It wasn't a particularly popular move with many of the squad, with a little bit extra put into some of the contact sessions in training, but, setting all that to one side, McWhirter had no doubt about Miller's quality.

'Eric was a strange individual,' he says. 'I'm not sure anybody [in Ulster] really knows him that well. I don't know whether he didn't buy into it or maybe it was just his form. When I first came across him it was an Ulster Schools v Leinster Schools, a game when Denis Hickie scored four tries. Eric was at eight for Leinster Schools. He had a really strong game even though he was a year younger than us. Everybody knew of him. He was a class footballer, a really, really good player.'

Despite the circumstances, Miller performed relatively well on his debut, even if his lack of match practice showed in the end, while the return of James Topping for the first time since he'd broken his collarbone on Ireland's summer tour to South Africa also provided a considerable boost to Williams who, if not for injury, would likely have hoped to start Topping on one wing and Tyrone Howe, still a teacher in England at the time, on the other.

Knowing they needed a try bonus and the victor at Donnybrook to win by a sizeable margin to secure the all-important top-two finish, things were going to plan when the hosts ran out to a 22–6 lead, but the crucial fourth try didn't arrive until Allen Clarke went over in the seventeenth minute.

With Munster securing the title by beating Leinster, the 25–10 scoreline saw the eastern province fail to bank a single match point and allowed Ulster to leapfrog them into second place. Whatever happened in the rest of their European campaign, Williams' men would at the very least be dining at the top table once again the next season.

With Ebbw Vale the next visitors to Belfast, it felt as though attention had already turned to Edinburgh in the final pool fixture, a game it seemed certain would decide who would finish as runner-up to Toulouse and bank a place in the last eight. Edinburgh were raising the ire of Ulster, and indeed Warren Gatland, thanks to their refusal to move the game from Sunday – the day the Ireland national team had planned to start a three-day training camp. Their reasoning was due to their arrangement with Hibs FC to play games at Easter Road, but the Scots stuck to their guns even after deciding to move the clash to the more intimate Myreside to create a more intimidating atmosphere. Relations were hardly helped when Ulster lodged an official complaint over the eligibility of Edinburgh's newly arrived Martin Leslie and scuppered his planned debut against Toulouse.

While Miller was never in the frame to take on Ebbw Vale, a substantial blow to the team's selection came when James Topping's luckless run continued with another fracture to his collarbone in training, one that would this time end his season, meaning Sheldon Coulter and McWhirter would both be restored to the starting line-up. With a point to prove, McWhirter wasted little time in making an impact as he and Andy Ward teamed up to ensure Ulster won the back-row battle. Ward was involved in all his side's tries, one of which was scored by a bursting McWhirter in a game that wasn't a classic but was always in hand.

The visitors were reduced to fourteen men with half an hour to go when Chay Billen struck Gary Longwell; a kerfuffle that, thanks to it occurring on the right wing, embroiled the undersized Sheldon Coulter. While he got a black eye for his trouble, he left nobody in any doubt that there was plenty of fight in even the smallest members of the Ulster squad. Overcoming one of David Humphreys' more inconsistent games when it came to kicking from hand and the ultimate rarity – an inaccurate day from Simon Mason off the tee – Ulster led 24–3 at half-time and 43–6 late on, but Ebbw Vale were allowed in for two late tries. The very last play of the game saw Tongan import Kuli Faletau, whose son Taulupe went on to play for Wales and the Lions, trundle over the line.

This pool better not come down to points difference, Williams thought to himself as his side headed for the showers.

13
MAKE OR BREAK

Few men had ever been more meticulous in their preparation for a day's work than Bill McLaren. The voice of rugby, the bard of the Borders, had always lived by the Scout motto of 'be prepared' and was an avid note taker over the course of fifty years of commentating for the BBC. Like any task, it got easier with time, even without the aid of the internet. After a few years on the beat, plenty of the research had been done two or three times over, with the relatively few rugby-playing nations only changing their playing panels gradually from season to season.

Every so often, though, the job threw a curveball, and it was one such occasion that brought him to Myreside the day before Edinburgh welcomed Ulster in what would be a winner-takes-all clash with a quarter-final spot on the line. As McLaren stood and watched the visitors' final training session before the pivotal encounter, it was clear – with his dog-eared notebook and variety of coloured pens – that he was on a fact-finding mission to aid his commentary on Harry Williams' low-profile squad.

'He didn't have a clue who half of us were,' says Jan Cunningham laughing. 'Obviously Humphreys and Wardy, but the rest of us he was asking coming off the pitch who we were and a bit about ourselves. He'd pull his notebook out of this tweed jacket and take it all down. He was legendary for this preparation, but he didn't have a clue about us. That's how it was – nobody did.'

If McLaren was quickly learning as much as he could about the Ulster squad, his BBC NI counterpart Jim Neilly was already daring to dream that they were on the verge of something special. Staying in the same hotel as the team, the much-loved commentator was leaving the lift when he bumped into tight head Rab Irwin heading back to his room.

'Rab, did you hear about Toulouse?' he asked excitedly. Irwin hadn't but didn't elaborate much further. 'They've been beaten by Ebbw Vale!'

The result was scarcely credible, not with the 1996 champions having put a hundred points on the Welsh side just two months before. Neilly continued. 'That means if you win tomorrow, you'll be home in the quarter-finals. Then if you can get a home draw in the semi-finals, you'll win that, and then the final would be in Lansdowne Road and then —'

'Let's just win tomorrow first, Jim,' Irwin interrupted.

Downstairs in the team room, the result was causing considerably more commotion, even if the players were still struggling to believe it. With only Teletext to go on, there was an assumption that some sort of error had been made. Looking for the definitive answer, Derick Topping rang directory enquiries and asked to be put through to the rugby club's bar. Putting on his best Welsh accent, the flanker, who was down to be on the bench the next day, explained that he'd been a fan all his life and was ringing to find out the score of the afternoon's game. The sound of the raucous party going on at the other end of the line told him everything he needed to know.

At that time Ulster knew nothing of the ugly scenes and violence that had marred the encounter, culminating in Scottish referee Ed Murray sending off prop Cyrille Vancheri, and Franck Tournaire accused of threatening behaviour towards an official in an exchange that saw a policeman's helmet knocked from his head. Whatever the circumstances, the upshot was the same: not only would the winner of the Edinburgh–Ulster clash be in the last eight, they would be hosting a quarter-final.

There was little doubt that a place in the knockouts would have been a huge boon to Scottish rugby, which had gone through something of an identity crisis over the previous eight months. Much like Ireland, when professionalism arrived the decision was taken that it wouldn't be prudent for Scotland's club sides to go head-to-head with the leading lights of France and England in European competition. Again, like their Celtic cousins, they were fortunate to have four traditional sides already at their disposal through the Scottish Inter-District Championship. While there was some rebranding done – The North and Midlands were renamed as Caledonia Reds while South of Scotland became Border Reivers – by and large it was the same four geographical districts that represented Scotland in their first years in Europe. By the spring of 1998, feeling unable to support upwards of a hundred professional players, the decision was taken to merge their four competing sides into two. As such, much to the distress of their national coach, Jim Telfer, Caledonia joined forces with Glasgow while the Reivers were subsumed by Edinburgh, leaving some forty players out in the cold. In their first year, there was little that was superlative about the so-called 'Super Districts', with Glasgow Caledonians finishing bottom of their pool after two wins from six. Edinburgh, meanwhile, had largely failed to impress but came into their final game with their two wins over Ebbw Vale and the draw with Ulster giving them a chance.

Edinburgh had played their previous European home games at Easter Road, the ground of Hibs football team, but because of a large visiting support made up of Ulster fans studying in Scotland, the game drew twice the crowd despite having been moved to the smaller Myreside.

The high-stakes contest began with Simon Mason and Craig Chalmers trading a pair of penalties before the hosts went on to score the next twelve points. With half an hour gone another Reivers penalty was sent to the corner and, with the superior line-out, they trucked the ball up a few times before a fine move that saw Alan Tait throw a miss pass to Iain Sinclair who put Tony Stanger away after the winger looped around the back. Their second try of the day arrived when, via another skip pass, Ulster were opened up for Cammie Murray to score in the corner. Craig Chalmers nailed the touchline conversion for an 18–6 lead.

A flu-ridden Allen Clarke had already departed when Tony McWhirter was felled and stretchered from the field with fifty-three minutes gone. Ulster's hopes of a quarter-final spot seemed as remote as they had done at any stage of the competition which, in itself, was no mean feat. Enter Derick Topping.

For Derick, some four years older than his Irish international brother James, rugby was certainly something that was in the family. The pair's father Fred was a forester and they had virtually grown up on Slieve Croob, a 1,750-foot mountain in County Down. Fred Topping had been instrumental in helping set up Ballynahinch Rugby Club, even constructing some of the pitches, but the family moved to Ballymena in the early 1980s and Eaton Park soon became home. The elder Topping brother had missed out on making a mark on the provincial set-up because he was at university in Leeds, but his chance came when he was back home in Ballymena in the summer of 1998. Andre Bester became his club coach and quickly adopted him as something of a cause célèbre. After the early struggles of Williams' side, Bester was on the phone hassling Williams to take a look at Topping and, eventually relenting, Williams selected Topping for his Ulster A debut against Munster in October. Topping made his senior bow soon after and had come off the bench away to Ebbw Vale for his only previous European outing.

On the biggest stage of his career, Derick had the game of his life and his introduction sparked life into Ulster.

'It was just one of those days,' he remembers. 'When you thought about that Toulouse result, you started to think something special might be happening, but then Edinburgh were no doubt thinking the same, especially when they were up 18–6. When I came off the bench, I hit off the line-out well from Gary Longwell and from there everything just seemed to go right. Balls bounced up for me, I was always in the right place at the right time no matter where I found myself on the pitch. You get games like that sometimes – they're the ones that really stick out when you look back on your career. I'd had a few for Ballymena the summer before and that was what probably made Andre Bester think I could do a job. That was when I was really just trying to stay in the Ballymena team, so to be playing for Ulster that soon, in a game like that, I really did feel incredibly lucky. It was nice afterwards to have people saying it was one of the performances that everybody sort of remembered, I suppose, but I was lucky. I just picked the right time to do it.'

With Topping to the fore, Ulster got back into things when Mark Blair, against a host of former teammates and just six miles from where he'd been turning out for Currie in his Scottish days, crashed over for a try. It was his Ballymena teammate, though, who would grab the headlines the next day: 'Shel done and dusted'.

Only twenty-one years old during the 1998–99 campaign, Sheldon Coulter had made his Ulster bow while still a teen. Attending Belfast Royal Academy, he'd been a promising footballer in his youth, playing in underage sides with the likes of Paul McKnight, who by 1998 was a Northern Ireland under twenty-one international on the books of Glasgow Rangers. Coulter's transformation into a rugby player was initially a slow process, but once he was convinced to help his school's medallion side he was soon brought into the Irish underage set-up, winning an under twenty-ones Triple Crown in 1996 as part of a side coached by fellow Ulsterman Brian McLaughlin.

Studying accountancy in Scotland, he'd been travelling back and forth to play for Ulster in his first year of university but was struck down with glandular fever not long after returning from his summer break. Faced with having to repeat the entire year, he took a break from his education only to be among the select few offered contracts for the first year of pro rugby at Ravenhill.

'I was sort of in limbo. I didn't really know what it was about, none of us did,' he says. 'My attitude was always to get my studies finished, that rugby was a hobby. There were no guarantees: when it came to Ireland they were learning as they went.

'Our first wage was still in punts but you were getting paid to do something that you enjoyed. You were all friends as well as colleagues.'

Ultimately deciding to put his studies on hold to give rugby his all, such was Coulter's form in 1997 that no less a figure than former Ireland and Lions fly half Tony Ward was using his *Evening Herald* column to campaign for an Ireland debut for him in that year's Five Nations. While the call from Brian Ashton never came, Coulter became a key figure for Harry Williams.

After scoring twice in the June contest with Spanish Barbarians, his early season was injury interrupted, but by the time the European campaign began he had displaced speedster Jonny Davis on the right wing, even if he occasionally found himself out of favour at Ballymena. The game plan at Eaton Park saw Bester preferring more sizeable men to Coulter – who was five foot eight and under twelve stone – out wide, opting for Kiwi Shane Stewart and even flanker Dean McCartney to fill the eleven and fourteen jerseys. That an Ulster wing couldn't crack his club side was the source of a jibe or two but Coulter wasn't one to pore over press cuttings. When he made his debut for Ballymena it was at centre, playing outside experienced number ten Derek McAleese. McAleese, who had scored all his side's points in Ireland's 44–12 defeat to France in 1992 – the only Test cap of his career – told the youngster never to read the newspapers, warning that not only could they turn you into a peacock one week and a feather duster the next, but that more often than not the reporter wouldn't even have been at the match in question.

After Myreside, there was nobody doubting Coulter's place in the side.

With sixty-nine minutes on the clock, another penalty from Chalmers was matched by Mason leaving the contest finely poised at 21–16. Ulster's second-half performance was much improved but the gig was up. Five points down, Edinburgh were about to seal the deal – all they had to do was exploit a three on one they had forced just inside the Ulster half. Coulter had already made one try-saving tackle minutes before but there was, it seemed, little he could do to save the day this time round. Under the circumstances, the diminutive winger gave it his best shot. As he looked up he saw Iain Sinclair coming towards him, the very same Iain Sinclair whose house he had stayed in when Belfast Royal Academy went on a school tour to Scotland. As the back rower tried to slip the telling pass through to Tait, Coulter went for broke, bursting through the lane and taking the ball in stride. Still some fifty metres from the line there was no catching him, not until he'd touched down underneath the posts to leave his full back with the simplest of conversions to break the 21–21 tie.

'When he got that ball … bang, he was away,' remembers Mason. 'Arguably that's the most crucial try of the whole season – one of Ulster's most important ever. That team wasn't always the superstars and Sheldon epitomised what Ulster was about. It's patronising the way people talked about him because he was a little lad but he gave everything. He worked hard, he was tireless. He summed up that idea that you create your own luck.'

The comeback was complete but the game was still to be

won with eleven minutes left and a considerable chunk of injury time to be added thanks to the lengthy treatment given to McWhirter. Having already suffered late heartache against Edinburgh once this season, the scene was set for similar last-gasp anguish. Duncan Hodge, the man behind the reverse fixture's drama, remained curiously on the bench in a game when one kick would have changed the entire course of their season and indeed the competition.

In his absence the burden of kicking responsibility fell on Chalmers' shoulders – no bad man to have your hopes resting upon, thought Edinburgh's coach, Ian Rankin. A Test Lion against the Australians in 1989, he was unfortunate Down Under after losing his place following their defeat in the opener, and subsequently missed out on the remainder of the come-from-behind series victory. Less than twelve months later he enjoyed his most enduring minutes on a rugby field as he and his Scotland teammates took a slow walk towards a Grand Slam title beating the England of Brian Moore, Will Carling and the rest, with Chalmers kicking nine oh-so-crucial points. For the remainder of the decade he and Gregor Townsend battled for the dark blue ten jersey, with Chalmers a game-managing ten compared to his more maverick rival.

Having started the game four from six off the tee, his missed drop goal as time sped past could have been consigned to a footnote of only the lengthiest of match reports after he stood over a penalty forty metres out with no time left. Ulster were helpless. Whether they progressed or not was no longer down to them. One swing of an opposition boot would decide their fate. The deflation was palpable; a side that had experienced defeat all too often in this competition could feel another only seconds away, one which, under the circumstances, would be the most gut-wrenching of the lot. Mark Blair, though, still hadn't lost a game when handed a starting jersey. He knew nothing of the many scars of past battles, nor did he ever assume he was about to. Standing underneath the posts, with his teammates hanging their heads, he confidently made a prediction: 'There's no chance he's getting this.'

Jan Cunningham looked up at him.

'No chance. I've seen plenty of him – out of his range, way out of his range.'

Not everyone was convinced.

'I thought he could have blown it over,' admits Williams.

Blair, it seems, knew what he was talking about: Chalmers' kick was closer to being a touch-finder than troubling the touch judge's flags. Ulster had won; Coulter was the hero.

'When I'm mentioned, that's the highlight,' he says. 'If it hadn't happened … what would have happened?'

What would have happened was Ulster's season would have been over in the first week of November. Instead they were in the quarter-finals and readying themselves to host Toulouse for the second time in a matter of months. The unforeseen and unprecedented events of the past twenty-four hours had caught everyone somewhat on the hop.

IRFU President Noel Murphy had been watching in Edinburgh, and soon after was asked by his Ulster counterpart, John Callaghan, what he should do in preparation for the staging of a knockout tie.

'For now, just purr like a cat,' he replied.

Despite the jubilation from the visitors, Edinburgh were understandably devastated and the wound didn't heal quickly. In 2008, as the prestigious Melrose Sevens tournament celebrated its 125th anniversary, Ulster entered a team in the over thirty-fives section that included the likes of Andy Ward, Stan McDowell, Andy Matchett and Rab Irwin. The contingent was in the bar on the first night of the weekend when Craig Chalmers came through the door and caught sight of the men who had ended his side's European dream almost a decade before. 'You bastards again,' he said, by way of a greeting.

The quarter-final would not be for over a month as provincial matters were put to one side and the focus quickly shifted to Ireland's upcoming games with Georgia and Romania and their bid to qualify for the 1999 Rugby World Cup. Allen Clarke, Jonny Bell and Andy Ward started all three, with Justin Fitzpatrick and David Humphreys as replacements. They'd all be back at Lansdowne Road sooner than anyone would ever dare to dream.

14
DELIVERY

'What are you doing here?'

A fair question, thought Andy Ward, even though the man was presumably referring to the waiting room of Lagan Valley's maternity ward rather than this small country half a world away from where he had grown up.

Of all the disparate stories that came together to form the Ulster Rugby squad's narrative of 1998–99, Ward's is perhaps the most far-fetched. Born in Whangerei on the tip of New Zealand's north island, Ward, whose family moved to Ohaupo when he was just four years old, grew up playing rugby barefoot at his local club, where players regimentally arranged themselves along the sideline – if not for any reasons of obedience then at least to warm their toes on the creosote used for pitch markings.

But it was initially BMX riding that was Ward's sporting priority; understandably so, given that he could make himself anywhere between one and two thousand New Zealand dollars a weekend while still at school. Having competed in two world championships, and with one top ten finish to his name, Ward laughs as he recalls, 'I made more money doing that than I ever thought I would or could from rugby. It paid for my first three cars.'

He came back to rugby later in his teens, making the development squad at Waikato, but progressed no further in his homeland, and a deal to move to Northern Ireland and play for Ballynahinch, then still a junior club, was arranged through a fellow Kiwi associated with Bangor. The switch only came about when the lock forward who was supposed to make the journey was injured in a workplace accident and, despite their more pressing need in the engine room, the County Down side agreed to take on a flanker instead.

What was first expected to be a short sojourn on the other side of the world turned on a chance encounter and a spot of car trouble. With his BMX income having dried up, Ward hadn't yet decided how best to make his way in the world. He was enjoying himself in a variety of odd jobs he'd picked up while on his travels. Some days he'd be outside all day, potting plants in a garden centre, others he'd spend cleaning the paintbrushes for Down High's art teachers before donning a tracksuit and assisting the PE department. He'd been driving to work on a sunny summer's day when his Peugeot got a flat tyre. With no jack, and in the days before mobile phones, his only hope was the kindness of strangers. The country roads that link County Down's moderately sized towns are hardly busy highways or byways, so Ward was relieved that the first door he knocked upon was opened and was even more reassured when he was told that of course he could make a call from the phone inside. A friend with the required tools to change the flat would be an hour in arriving, so, like all good Kiwi boys, he made the most of the rare opportunity to get some sun. Sitting on the bonnet of his stricken vehicle with his shirt discarded as he enjoyed the rays, he soon had company for the wait.

'All I heard was the squeak of the door and the rattle of a tray,' he says. 'The next thing these two old ladies, two sisters, came down with a pot of tea and sandwiches. We sat together having a great day's craic, talking about this, that, and the other.'

Not long after, and quicker than he would have liked, Ward found his stint in the northern hemisphere was up and he returned home to his family and friends. Far from being greeted as a prodigal son, he was taking the short stroll to his local pub, offering greetings to those he passed on the way, when he was struck by an epiphany.

'There was a fella in his garden, weeding away, and it was a cracking morning. I just said to him, "G'morning." No acknowledgement, nothing, didn't even look up. I said hello to the next person I saw, same thing, didn't look up at me. I just thought to myself, if I had been in Ireland, where those two old ladies who didn't know me from Adam took the time to spend the whole afternoon with me, how different that morning would have been. That summed up Ulster and its people to me.

'My mind was made up. I finished walking to the pub, told the boys, "Bollocks to this, I'm going back," and that was that, the rest is history. The next twenty-four, twenty-five years have been down to those two old ladies.'

Back in Ballynahinch, as the club rose rapidly through the ranks, so too did Ward. In the days before imports stepped off the plane one day and pulled on the red hand the next, he came on to the provincial radar long before he could be selected for the side thanks to his standout performances at Ballymacarn Park. Flashy and skilled, yet with more ability on the deck than he was sometimes given credit for, Ward was all the more noticeable for his brightly coloured scrum cap. He made his Ulster debut in 1997. He was the province's first adopted son in the days before those born in the nine counties could sometimes be found in the minority in the starting side.

Just like at his beloved Ballynahinch, it wasn't long before he was seen as a talismanic figure for the province and, by the spring of 1998, he was given an Ireland bow by fellow former Waikato man Warren Gatland for the Five Nations clash with France. His first experience of pulling on the green jersey would be a losing one, as was so often the case in that era for the Irish against Les Bleus, but despite the need for one deep breath as the team bus pulled into the Stade de France, Ward held his own and his place for the rest of the campaign and into the summer tour to South Africa.

As such, he was Ulster's sole international that season, pulling on the green jersey months before the influx of Test-level talent flooded back to Ravenhill. Now joined by better players, his star shone no less bright and he remained both a key figure and a favourite of the fans. Harry Williams was overjoyed to find a back rower who seemed happy to run the whole game and then all the way home if you'd let him.

'You couldn't be tired,' says Ward, whose future lay in the fitness industry. 'We were still playing for the clubs then, so I'd train with Ulster, and when we weren't, I'd train for Hinch. You'd play Friday, then if required you'd play Saturday for the club and I'd go for a ten kilometre run on a Sunday. I always had it in my head that the fitter you are the less injuries you get, so I tried to stay flat out all the time. If I hadn't been a professional rugby player, I'd have been doing the same. It's just how I was, how I still am.'

If Simon Mason's metronomic boot grabbed the headlines, and Humphreys ability for breathtaking moments of brilliance provided the belief that anything was possible, then Ward was the team's steady heartbeat. Understandably, there was palpable apprehension, even disbelief, when it emerged his participation in the quarter-final was under threat. He and his wife Wendy – whom he had met through a friend of a friend in the rugby club – were expecting their first baby the week before the game. They had decided months before, back when the prospect of rugby still being played in Belfast so close to Christmas seemed a laughable prospect, that he would be present to welcome their first child into the world no matter what. Knowing that the crucial call could come at any moment, Ward trained throughout the week but, ahead of what was the province's most important game in decades, found his mind wandering as he went through moves on the paddock. He'd missed only one game the entire season, the heavy defeat to Toulouse out in France, but despite Harry Williams telling him the decision was his, as was the number seven jersey should he choose to fill it, all week he'd had the nagging suspicion that he'd miss the game. There were things more important than rugby – even European Cup quarter-final rugby.

There were other selection headaches for Williams to ponder. Centre Clinton van Rensburg had by then departed for a full contract on offer at Swansea, and despite Ulster's best efforts his Welsh employers, who weren't in European action, wouldn't release the South African for the quarter-final. Meanwhile, a shoulder injury sustained by Stephen Bell during a Dungannon training session he attended for the sole purpose of working through the frustrations of not being selected for Ireland A ruled him out too. Neil Doak, an Irish international cricketer who once took the wicket of Brian Lara, had once seemed destined to represent Ireland in rugby too. He'd sat on the bench without ever having his number called, and had gone to the 1995 World Cup without seeing the pitch, but he'd endured lengthy injury travails of late. It meant Mark Edwards was called on to the bench behind Andy Matchett, joining his Bective Rangers half-back partner Bryn Cunningham among the replacements. But it was still the possibility of sending his troops into battle without Ward, one of their key leaders, that was giving the coach most cause for consternation.

The much-feared possibility seemed a certainty when Wendy, now a full seven days overdue, was booked in to be induced on Friday, the very morning, as it happened, that Toulouse were in town with revenge on their minds. Derick Topping, who had played so well when called on against Edinburgh in the game which lifted Ulster to this unforeseen point, had already been told to prepare himself when the day's papers landed on doorsteps to inform fans of the news they had feared all week: Ward would not play.

'What are you doing here?' asked gynaecologist Michael Crooks with more than a hint of self-interest, for the doctor himself had tickets to the game that would kick off in some ten hours' time. Crooks, a huge rugby fan, couldn't wrap his head around the sight of one of Ulster's key men sitting in the waiting room reading a newspaper when he should have been preparing for the visit of French giants.

As Ward is at pains to point out during the many requested retellings of this almost cinematic tale, the doctor would never have made mother and baby anything less than the number one priority; still, after spending the first minutes of the conversation apologising that the hospital planned such a procedure at such a time, Mr Crooks' attention quickly shifted to a plan of action. Feeling there'd be no harm in trying to speed the process along a little, he instructed the midwives to do all they could to ensure the newborn would arrive in time for lunch rather than dinner. He swung into the room requesting an update each hour, always hoping to hear that the labour process had begun, but as the minutes ticked away with no movement, a change of tack was required. Having originally wanted to ensure the baby came as quickly as possible, come mid-afternoon there was no prospect of that. The midwives were now told to slow the process to a crawl, with any luck delaying the birth until after the game.

Ward was initially sceptical, but one look at Wendy and he knew he had her support to take a brief leave of absence. Quickly he found himself behind the wheel and on the road to Ravenhill, negotiating his way through rush-hour traffic. Captain David Humphreys was the first to hear the flanker would be playing after all, or at the very least starting the game before hotfooting it back to Lagan Valley. Instructions and a phone were left with Mark McCall who was to act as a conduit between stadium and hospital. He was told in no uncertain terms to call Ward ashore as soon as it became clear his presence was required elsewhere. When he arrived into the changing room less than an hour before kick-off, Ward was greeted like a long-lost friend with the flurry of cheers and backslapping giving the whole squad a boost just as they were ready to go out for their final warm-up. If Ulster were to go down, at least they would do so with a full arsenal at their disposal.

15
CHRISTMAS COMES EARLY

While the will-he-won't-he Andy Ward saga offered a theatrical subplot to the quarter-final build-up, French visitors Toulouse were involved in melodramas of their own. Having been beaten in Belfast already during the campaign, it was a case of once bitten, twice shy. There were to be no tentative team selections this time around, and eight weeks on from their first visit, the fifteen selected by Guy Novès included nine French internationals as well as the New Zealander Lee Stensness.

The Kiwi's eligibility for the tie was called into question amid accusations he'd still been playing for Auckland beyond the European Cup's registration deadline. An All Black who made his Test debut against the British and Irish Lions in 1993, the availability of the centre provided a boost to the already confident visitors, but there was plenty of further sweating to be done. The fallout from their ill-tempered defeat to Ebbw Vale earlier in the year – the very reason the last eight tie was being played in Ravenhill rather than the south of France – had dragged all the way to the eve of the side's planned departure, with Franck Tournaire facing a disciplinary hearing that was expected to see the prop handed a ban that would rule him out of the game. The self-styled bad boy of French rugby, Tournaire would soon be in hot water again when accused of biting All Blacks captain Taine Randell in a World Cup semi-final. On this particular occasion it was his involvement in the spat with touch judge Rob Dickson that was at the centre of the storm. Much to the rugby world's surprise, however, the prop's behaviour was found to be 'unnecessary but not threatening', with the club fined only £2,600. Ray Harris, the Ebbw Vale CEO, described himself as 'dumbfounded by the leniency', but the bottom line was that Toulouse travelled in the expectation of having a full deck to choose from, including devastating wing Émile Ntamack, who had overcome a hamstring injury to take his place in the travelling party, and Tournaire's partner in crime, Christian Califano, fit for the first time that European season. No wonder Novès arrived in a confident mood.

'We will win,' he said, with little thought seemingly given to launching a local charm offensive. 'We will play a better game than last time. We were very annoyed that in the end we have to travel in the quarter-finals. That was not our intention.'

Harry Williams for one wasted little time in seeing to it that home comforts, indeed, had been left behind.

'Ahh, they weren't happy at all when they arrived,' says Simon Mason. 'We'd already beaten them in Belfast, which probably didn't help, and then you had Harry who always had a bit of mischief. They were flying into Belfast and Harry's giving it the "They'll be getting a delay through customs" and a wink to anyone who'll listen. It probably wasn't even true but the players believed it anyway.'

On their first visit to Belfast earlier in the year, Toulouse had been able to make use of the facilities at Cooke RFC – the club located on Shaw's Bridge, a stone's throw from the city centre. The Ulster Branch policy was to rotate visiting European sides through the neighbouring clubs for training purposes, so this time it was decided that the team becoming known as the artisans of European rugby would be handed the keys to the more rural Ballymacarn Park in Ballynahinch. Around twenty miles from Belfast, the French side believed this to be some sort of high jinks perpetrated by their previously welcoming hosts and were quick to make their objections known, even if they were later withdrawn.

Eventually reassured that there was nothing untoward about their given training facilities, the team were left in little doubt that mischief was at play when they arrived at Ravenhill. With Ravenhill having two changing rooms of sufficient size to house a burly squad of rugby players and their kit, it was presumed, naturally enough, that the sides would each take one for the quarter-final. That wasn't possible, however, thanks to the unusual and unprecedented decision from Ulster to turn the customary away dressing room into a media centre. There were, they argued, many more journalists than usual to accommodate even though, in truth, it was believed that a date clash with the annual Bass Brewery Christmas party had actually depleted the numbers.

Toulouse were given two smaller rooms, splitting their squad and raising French ire. As Simon Mason ducked under the stand after his kicking practice, he arrived into the middle of all hell breaking loose in the tight corridor. 'Pandemonium, absolute pandemonium,' says the full back, laughing as he remembers the sight of the Toulouse twenty-five crowded into what was intended as a room for four referees. 'Mayhem. I think they probably changed the regulations off the back of it.'

By the time kick-off rolled around twelve thousand were crammed into Ravenhill, the first time the home of Ulster Rugby had witnessed a sell-out since the All Blacks were in town in 1989. The rain was horizontal while the wind swirled, the conditions so poor that even Mason struggled with his first effort off the tee. But with Ulster's forwards up and into the faces of their French counterparts, the pressure on the handling skills of Toulouse was relentless. Ward, despite the distractions, was still to the fore. If his mad dash to the game already seemed the stuff of folklore, his hero status was further cemented when he did his best Superman impression with a fully extended flying tackle on Michael Marfaing along the touchline. The first try was agonisingly close when Humphreys was just beaten to the ball by the chasing Romuald Paillat at a time when winning the foot race would have brought a score, but the same man's sweetly struck drop goal shortly after gave the hosts the first points.

A long-range penalty from Mason fell just short, while another drop goal attempt from Humphreys, this time from the touchline, didn't find its target either, but Ulster were throwing everything at the task. Forwards buzzed into contact, while backs were quick to join them, and the accuracy of the Allen Clarke to Gary Longwell connection in the line-out defied the conditions to offer an attacking platform.

For all the questions asked of his defence, Mason stopped a rampaging Stensness with an excellent tap tackle, supported quickly by Andy Park, Stephen McKinty and Clarke, who dragged the prone All Black across the sideline. When Toulouse came into the Ulster line-out from the side, Mason's measured penalty doubled the lead, giving the full back a century of points in the competition.

Boosted by his involvement in the tackle that set up the second penalty, Park was buzzing around the pitch, having come on as an early replacement for the injured Stan McDowell. 'You do always prefer to start because you can prepare properly,' he says of his much earlier than anticipated arrival. 'Irrespective of what anyone says, it's not the same from the bench. You're sitting there in your big coat thinking you want to be playing. But Stanley got injured against Toulouse and you go to warm up thinking about how, in a game like that, you don't want to be the one who lets people down. You don't want to be that guy and it focuses your mind. The adrenaline kicks in and you're either going to perform or you're a rabbit in the headlights.

Our game was quite limited, let's be honest, so there wasn't that much to focus on. It was just a case of don't let the guys down, but you have to keep that concentration because you can be exposed on the wing.'

There was little danger of that on the night in question as Park, for all the size of him, was described as a 'dog with a bone' by a watching reporter as he harried Xavier Garbajosa into touch, setting up another Humphreys' drop goal. At 9–0 up, Ravenhill dared to dream.

Half-time came and, while Ward dealt with a dislocated thumb, there was still no word to say he was required back at the hospital. With everything going to script, even if it was a script that'd be rejected as fanciful by film-makers, Ulster grew in stature with every hit, every turnover, and, of course, every point from the boot of Mason or Humphreys. Finally, six minutes into the second half, Toulouse registered their first points of the contest through a Delaigue penalty.

Then came the call that anyone with a drop of Ulster blood coursing through their veins had hoped and prayed would be delayed just that little bit longer. 'The rules of me playing were that I had my own phone with me, and gave it to Mark McCall,' says Ward. 'I told him "Smally, if that phone rings, I have to go, no matter what." We got to half-time, and we were up, we're coming off then and everything is going to plan, everyone is playing well and it's a serious atmosphere. Ten minutes into the second half and the phone call comes. John Martin our physio said to Smally "Don't tell him. We can't have him off now". They had this massive argument for about five minutes while they waited for the ball to go dead but Smally told him he'd promised me and that was that.'

As Ward dashed from the field, touching his own hand to the red one emblazoned on his chest, the crowd roared him down the tunnel.

Ward was standing briefly in the shower, trying to ensure

his first child wasn't welcomed into the world in mud-soaked, rain-lashed arms, when the face of Ronnie Flanagan, the RUC's chief constable, appeared from behind the corner. Sir Ronnie, as he was to become following the New Year's Honours List later that same month, was no stranger to rugby, having turned out for the province alongside the likes of Mike Gibson, Willie John McBride and Dick Milliken. As part of a CIYMS side who were accused of veering dangerously close to professionalism when they accepted the prize of Parker fountain pens for winning an annual tournament in Bangor, Flanagan must have found this spectacle – the paid players doing battle in European competition – an alien concept, but he wasn't about to see a fellow Ulsterman stuck. He suggested that his car and driver, waiting outside the stadium, would be the fastest way for Ward to get to the hospital. While this no doubt proved to be the case, the ten miles traversed in just thirteen minutes, Ward was given the fright no prospective father needs on one of the biggest days of his life when the peaks and troughs of the Hillhall Road caused a machine gun to bounce from under the passenger seat.

'Is the safety on this at least?' he nervously asked the driver.

'Just put your foot on it,' he was told.

With Derick Topping thrown into the mix, Ulster's lead didn't dissipate in Ward's absence. Instead, a further two penalties from Mason stretched the score to 15–3. However, the French were too good a side to go meekly into the night and any sense of calm was all but obliterated by the final quarter.

Delaigue's second penalty of the contest reduced the arrears to nine points with twenty-five minutes to go, before the game's only try came twelve minutes from time. If Toulouse's catch and drive from a close-range line-out left fingernails bitten and nerves shredded, the scorer, lock Fabien Pelous, appeared to think the result, and his side's progression to the final four, was a foregone conclusion. As he crashed over, the French international, who was then thirty-three caps into a Test career that would ultimately see him retire as Les Bleus' most capped player, winked at the crowd in celebration, appearing to mouth, 'It's over, it's over' in the direction of Gary Longwell. The strength of this contention was no doubt only hardened when his full back, Stéphane Ougier, nailed the conversion from the touchline. Two points in arrears and with a couple of clock ticks over ten minutes to get them, momentum was with the visitors. Ulster, meanwhile, were in uncharted waters and were feeling the weight of history. A late defeat to a side who had never missed out on the semi-finals would have been far and away Ulster's most memorable campaign, the sort of hard-luck losers' tale that was Irish rugby's stock-in-trade in the era. And so it looked sure to be when Humphreys chipped ahead and, to his horror, saw the ball fielded by Ougier. An engineer by trade, Ougier had won four French caps spread over five years but was one of the unheralded members of Toulouse's backline. While he'd missed out on the recent success enjoyed by Les Bleus, he had played, and indeed scored, in the first-ever European clash, a Tuesday afternoon game hosted by Farul Constanța of Romania, with only three thousand spectators there to bear witness. Having lined out in that year's final too – Toulouse's win over Cardiff in Arms Park – he could be considered a veteran of these occasions, if such status was possible in only the competition's fourth edition.

Ougier was calmness personified as he strode forward and set Marfaing haring up the sideline. Capable of playing ten, centre or wing, Marfaing had made his international debut in the same 1992 Test as Ougier but, like his backline accomplice, had found himself on the outside looking in when it came to French selection. It was not, presumably, anything to do with his try-scoring record – by the time he retired nobody would have more European tries to their name, and he'd already accounted for seven that season, including four in the record rout of Ebbw Vale to open the campaign. Clinical to the point of coldly efficient, there was sure to be only one result when he looked up and saw nothing but an expanse of green in front of him.

As Marfaing set off like a gazelle across the Serengeti, Mason cursed that he hadn't stopped the move in its tracks seconds earlier, thinking that for all he'd done during the year a missed tackle might be his last act. It looked for all the world as though Jan Cunningham was the last hope as he tried to work the angle into the corner from the periphery but, despite seventy-eight draining minutes sapping his legs, it was Humphreys who somehow got across as if from nowhere to make the most famous tackle in Ulster Rugby's history – an intervention all the more memorable given who made it.

'I didn't make too many so I guess that's why that one sticks in everyone's mind so much,' says Humphreys, drily. 'I tried to avoid tackling more than anything else. It just seemed like the kind of thing that you'd hurt yourself doing.'

And so it proved, for by the time Ravenhill's elation at the unlikely survival of the narrow lead subsided, the roar had been replaced with an almost eerie silence at the sight of Humphreys still prone on the ground and clutching his shoulder. Team doctor David Irwin was first on the scene confirming what the pain etched on Humphreys' face had already revealed – his quarter-final was over.

Ulster's third captain of the season departed down the tunnel with a tear in his eye, believing that if his side were to play in the semi-finals, he wouldn't be there with them; a once in a lifetime opportunity would pass him by. In the changing room underneath the old stand with a sprained AC joint, white as a sheet and lost in his own world for a few seconds, the team's star was inconsolable by the time his father, mother and wife arrived to assess the damage. George Humphreys, a doctor by trade, took one look at his eldest son and confidently told him he'd be fine for any last-four clash ... as long as his teammates could get there without him. With no television in the vicinity, all the

Humphreys clan could do was listen, using the crowd as their guide. Sitting on the cold and unforgiving wood of the benches, a jagged pain still digging into his shoulder joint, Humphreys waited for that one last, long cheer that would mean the final whistle.

In Humphreys' stead, Williams called upon twenty-year-old Bryn Cunningham. A gifted junior sportsman, Cunningham had excelled at tennis before ultimately deciding on rugby and had been turning out for Bective Rangers while at university in Dublin. It was his first Ulster outing since coming from the bench in the loss to Leinster three months prior, and what followed were by far the most important two minutes of his rugby-playing life. As he waited to enter the fray, his fresh face and youthful good looks betrayed his inexperience.

'If I was a nineteen- or twenty-year-old today, it probably wouldn't seem as bad,' Cunningham says. 'The game has moved on so much that guys coming out of school, some of them are already physically and mentally developed enough to go straight in at that level. You see guys making senior and even international debuts at that age. But back then it was unheard of. I felt like the baby of that entire group. I physically wasn't developed in the slightest – I'd never had weight training at school or anything. I was very slight and you looked across at the French teams and they were huge. There was a nervousness there that was just about whether you'd be able to survive.'

Coming into that environment was no doubt a challenge, even more so given the importance of the man he'd just replaced.

'You had a massive inferiority complex back then,' he says. 'If guys had been playing over in the Premiership, they were gods. It seemed a world away from what we were playing locally. You watched *Rugby Special* at the weekends and it was all geared to English clubs. The fact that they'd been over there and played, it made them seem on a different level. And, to be honest, a lot of the time they were. Professionalism over there had kicked in earlier and those extra two or three years had made a huge difference. Their conditioning was certainly on a different level and David was a talismanic figure as well. He drove everything on and off the pitch. An obviously unbelievable player and then his backup was this unproven, wispy fella who'd played very little rugby. It was a big shift.

'You just didn't go through your squad then in the same way as there weren't the same injuries. You had your starting team and you didn't really use your bench, so I would go seasons without getting off the bench in those days, and then you're in a European Cup quarter-final against Toulouse. You had to just rely on your brain to see you through. I used mine as best as I could to make sure I only touched the ball about twice.'

Cool heads were required but with the atmosphere at fever pitch there was barely a chance to hear a thought rattle in your head. What Williams would have given to have had Humphreys, McCall or Ward on the pitch to calm the other players. In the end, the burden of responsibility fell on his scrum half, Andy Matchett.

Needing to negotiate a scrum deep in their own territory, the first instinct was to have Tony McWhirter wheel from the base, still a legal practice in 1998, and ebb away as many seconds as possible. Eventually, though, the ball would have to be played and Matchett was charged with deciding the plan of action.

'Matchy, what's the plan?' shouted Jonny Bell from the centre. No response.

'Matchy, what's the plan?' he shouted again, a little louder this time in an effort to be heard over the din of the crowd.

Still nothing.

'Matc—'

'Dinger, shut the fuck up and give me a second here,' snapped the scrum half.

In the end Ulster kicked up the touchline and trusted their defence to hold out for just one more set.

For the second game in a row, it came down to a kick at the death but Delaigue's effort, like that of Craig Chalmers' before him, was skewed from the start and didn't trouble the posts. Twelve thousand pairs of lungs breathed a collective sigh of relief. The shrill blast of Brian Campsall's final whistle pierced the air soon after and the raucous cheer told the pacing Humphreys that his side had somehow hung on. As Garbajosa slumped against a post with a look of disbelief, fans swarmed past the elegant winger and on to the pitch to share in the magic as players donned Santa hats in celebration and chants of 'Olé, olé, olé' filled the air.

It was the biggest win at the famous old ground since the Wallabies were beaten in 1984 – a game that also finished 15–13 thanks to full back Philip Rainey having kicked his side to victory. But through the rejoicing only one man recognised that this most glorious of nights was just the beginning.

In the coming weeks, borrowing a trait employed by Sir Alex Ferguson, the Manchester United manager in the middle of a historic treble-winning season, Harry Williams banned his players from touching the European trophy when it arrived in Dublin for photo-calls. They could get their hands on it, he said, only once they'd earned the right to do so. For all such talk, though, the wily coach went home and told his wife that he thought their name was already on the cup.

In Lagan Valley's maternity wing, midwives had been watching the match on the hospital's television and giving Andy Ward regular updates on the proceedings. Just shy of ten o'clock, Zachary Ward was born, the son of a European Cup semi-finalist. Fatherhood, though, didn't keep Ward from the team's Christmas party a couple of days after their monumental win. While there were some notable abstainers, such as Humphreys, who had never drunk, and Longwell, who by then had decided to give it up, Williams' squad were known to enjoy a drink when the occasion merited it – that tended to be every Wednesday in The Bot followed by The Fly. The festive party of 1998 was certainly seen as a special night, though.

The first casualty of the evening was Simon Mason's Armani shirt, a two-hundred-pound relic of his days at high-paying Richmond. Harry Williams didn't approve of it and the shirt was soon ripped to shreds, buttons spraying across Shaftesbury Square. The ripped Armani shirt started something of a theme as come closing time players wrestled the shirts from each other's backs. In all the hubbub, a few players returned from a tactical visit to Julie's Kitchen to find the police attending the scene. Thankfully the players were able to convince the coppers that it was all in good fun and that the man trapped under a chair was indeed a teammate rather than a genuine captive. When another player, one who was carrying an injury no less, was seen sprinting into the distance trying to jump over cars, Williams came out to survey the scene. The team looked nervously at their boss, trying to gauge his reaction.

'I'm counting that as a passed fitness test,' he muttered.

16
RAVENHILL RENOVATIONS

In the 1850s, some decades after an English schoolboy named William Webb Ellis picked up the ball and began to run, the fledgling roots of rugby football began to spread throughout Ireland, though the city of Belfast remained blissfully unaware of the burgeoning sport.

The first rugby football club formed on the island was at Trinity in 1854, largely thought to be a result of boys returning home after time spent in the English public-school system. With no opposition to play, the first games tended to be inter-squad tussles at the Dublin academic institution, with the players organised in alphabetical order or with English-educated pupils against their Irish equivalents. While schools in Dungannon and Enniskillen were early adopters, the game didn't make a dent in cricket's supremacy in Belfast until a rugby section was formed by the North of Ireland Cricket Club in 1868. When Queen's University did likewise in the autumn of 1869, a game between the two was arranged for the following January. It took place at Ormeau and took three separate Saturdays of play to complete. Queen's proved victorious, which was just as well given that they fielded eighteen players to the thirteen from North. In the decade that followed, the establishment of clubs such as Windsor,

Belmont and Albion, all of which have now fallen by the wayside, gave birth to a thriving rugby scene in Ulster's largest city.

When the date of the first interprovincial was set for 27 November 1875, and the fixture confirmed to be Ulster against Leinster at Ormeau, of the twenty players selected by the hosts, all represented clubs based in Belfast, and the thousand spectators who turned out to cheer them on was a new record for the sport in the city. From that day forward, and from those humble beginnings, an Ulster Rugby side, wearing a white jersey emblazoned with a red hand – the strip that they wore on that very first outing – would be a continuous presence in Belfast, eventually finding their home at Ravenhill in the south-east of the city. But in all the years since, there was never an occasion quite like the one that took place on 9 January 1998.

Moments after Ulster had beaten Toulouse in the last eight, long before the crowd had begun to file out onto the streets of Mount Merrion and Onslow Parade, planning had begun for the semi-final. For all the goodwill engendered by the developing fairy tale, if the Irish side were to be drawn at home, logistics were always going to prove an issue. The twelve thousand spectators packed into Ravenhill that night were the biggest numbers for a decade, but a last-four clash would require space for at least an additional eight thousand more.

With Ulster versus Toulouse the first of the last eight ties, the rest of the weekend was spent watching to see who would join the province in the semi-finals. Saturday saw France dominate Wales as Perpignan beat Llanelli and Stade Français humbled Pontypridd with a score of 71–14. Come Sunday, the dream of an all-Irish final died as Munster fell to Colomiers at the Stade Selery. Having won the French Rugby Union Championship the year before, and having preceded their thumping of Pontypridd with five pool wins from six, Parisian outfit Stade were the side everyone wanted to avoid. Or rather, almost everyone.

'I called Harry Williams as soon as I heard we drew Stade

and we were telling each other it was the best draw you could have asked for,' remembers Allen Clarke, who despite coming off with a calf problem against Toulouse would be ready for the semi-final. 'You were always going to have to beat them at some stage if you were going to win the trophy and, for us, our best chance was to get them at Ravenhill. The way they played the game, we were far better off getting them in the semi-finals.'

Clarke's point of view, it seemed, was shared in French rugby circles. Stade – despite their big quarter-final win, the return of their previously ineligible talisman Diego Dominguez and the presence of the Bouclier de Brennus in their trophy cabinet – made it clear they were looking forward to a weekend in Belfast as much as a sugar addict looks forward to a dentist appointment.

With the other semi-final an all-French affair between Colomiers and Perpignan, a double-header with Stade's game as the aperitif was a dream scenario for those working in French television, but one that was only possible should both games kick-off on the Saturday. Meanwhile, there were concerns about how Ulster could sufficiently increase capacity at Ravenhill, especially given what had happened at the Armand Césari Stadium in 1992. There, the Corsican minnows SC Bastia had looked to take advantage of the visit of a Marseille side, then one of the best in Europe. Tragically the stadium added extra seating only for a temporary stand to collapse killing eighteen and injuring many hundreds more.

Seemingly offended by the very idea of playing on a Friday night, and sceptical that Ravenhill could be safely transformed into a venue with the capacity for twenty thousand people, Stade president Max Guazzini, a communications magnate who had pumped millions into the club, made his frustrations known in a fax to EPCR chairman Roger Pickering:

> You have refused our request that the match against Ulster be played on Saturday January 17. As a consequence, you are

preventing the match being transmitted live on television in France even though French Rugby has played an important part in this competition. Your decision also denies France television from transmitting one of the most important matches in the competition despite France television's considerable financial contribution through their purchase of television rights. We do not fear playing at Ravenhill but we do not accept that your decisions should be determined by the particular interests of one party.

It was clear there would be a keen Parisian eye watching over proceedings as Ulster attempted to drag Ravenhill up to code and keep the game in Belfast.

Enter Mike Reid. Ulster's chief executive was a rugby man to his core – his father Ken has been described as one of Ireland's most renowned and innovative sports administrators. The elder Reid had served as president and secretary of both the Ulster Branch and the IRFU, as well as a selector and team manager for the national side; the latter post held during the 1991 World Cup when Ireland came so close to causing a historic upset against Australia. A titanic figure of the game in Ulster, he was the patriarch of a sporting family even if Mike's contributions prior to 1997 had largely gone unnoticed.

'There was an article that the venerable Ned Van Esbeck wrote about our family: my father and all his rugby prowess, my mum who played hockey at Stranmillis, my brother who played Irish Schools and then a full stop,' said Reid Jnr laughing. 'I didn't get a mention but I always loved sport, all sport really.'

Ken Reid, the son of an RUC officer, was born in Derry, but he started his secondary school education at Down High in Downpatick before moving to south Belfast's Methodist College, the school that his sons would later attend. By then Saturdays spent at Deramore, the home of Collegians, were already a ritual for Reid Jnr. As he progressed into the senior side, he was one of a host of like-minded clubmen who, thanks to their own playing commitments, found themselves either unable to attend Ulster games or arriving late and spending the afternoon in the bar underneath the stand. His career at Northern Bank and the arrival of four children put further constraints on his time. Seeing Ulster at Ravenhill on a Saturday afternoon became a rarity and, judging by the size of the crowd through the turnstiles in the last decade of the millennium, the same was true for many others.

It was something that played on Reid's mind when, still only in his mid-thirties, he was made aware of the upcoming advertisement for the position of the first-ever chief executive of the Ulster Branch. His father had warned him that any application with Reid written on it would be received with healthy fears of nepotism, but after considering the criteria he still decided to throw his hat in the ring. In the summer of 1997, the twin problems facing the branch were a poor financial year the season past and the very pressing need to bring more fans, whether veterans or new faces, into Ravenhill. The job therefore required someone with a head for both numbers and brand building. Who better, Reid thought to himself, than someone who had spent seventeen years working in banking, the last five of which were in the marketing department. Regardless of his family tree, the Ulster Branch agreed, even if landing the gig proved to be only the start of the battle.

'It's funny,' he remembers. 'When I got that job I was thirty-six. When I went for the interview I think they almost thought I was too young. My dad nearly told me not to go for it because he said there'd be accusations that I was just my father's son, but they were after someone with a financial background and a marketing background.

'I had done accountancy originally – I had been a business banker with Northern Bank and then the five years after I had been a small business marketing manager. It felt like the job was written for me, but it was a very different organisation I was going into back then. It was a small business, with a turnover of £200,000 and four members of staff.'

With contracted staff so thin on the ground, even rarer than the lesser-spotted full-time player, by its very design the Ulster Branch was set up to make use of the goodwill and any available free time of a committed band of volunteers. While they were the lifeblood of the organisation, the volunteer-led committees, with their multiple strata of governance, hardly lent themselves to swift and decisive action, especially given apprehension over the break with tradition represented by a CEO wielding such power. Reid's appointment was met with more than a degree of friction.

Undeterred and buoyed by the courage of his convictions, Reid started his own version of revolution with gusto, all geared towards making Ulster Rugby a financially viable and professional operation. Even though it was one that hadn't hitherto existed, the position was a dream job and Reid's enthusiasm, as well as the changing face of the game, did much to chip away any opposition to his ideas. Long before he'd even had time to arrange the layout of his office, which given the organised chaos he preferred for his desk would matter little anyway, he was out on the road looking for inspiration. Visits to London Irish and Northampton were eye-openers. Reid's key observations were that the two main strategies were Friday night games and the fostering of a family-friendly environment. For a man who found himself thinking 'Why not?' more often than 'Why?', taking the best of both seemed a natural plan.

The switch to Friday nights, which had been tentatively road-tested in recent seasons, immediately widened the pool of potential fans, while the idea of generating a sporting event for the whole family placed Ulster in a relatively unique position in Belfast's sporting landscape. Even when enjoying their most successful period, qualifying for back-to-back World Cups under Billy Bingham in 1982 and 1986, the national football side would always carry something of a political or religious connotation for some. Just off the staunchly loyalist Sandy Row, Windsor Park could feel unwelcoming, even dangerous, to Catholics, despite their religious background being far better represented in that particular green jersey than on the field at Ravenhill. Similarly, there were Protestants who would never have felt comfortable turning towards the Irish tricolour on northern soil or who were unable to overlook the GAA's seeming glorification of IRA members through the naming of clubs or grounds.

Rugby, which had always operated on an all-island basis, even when separate unions were coexisting in both Belfast and Dublin, was in a prime position to pitch itself somewhere in the middle. With considerably fewer political connotations, and certainly lacking the threat of violence that was still associated with football terraces, for Reid the marketing seemed obvious.

'The Ulster Branch was changing in dynamic,' he recalls. 'There were a lot of strong characters who were going. The McKibbins, Des and Harry, Noel Henderson, my father, strong characters were going and there was a new dynamic that was very open to change. A professional sport couldn't be paid for with two hundred spectators, that much was obvious to everyone, so that was why they needed the two strands – marketing and finance. In those days there was a huge crowd playing and watching rugby at club level and schools' level, so there was that ready-made market for it, but in 1996–97 they couldn't get to games on a Saturday. Also, there was nothing else happening in Northern Ireland really, so there was an opportunity to get new fans in too. Northern Ireland of the mid-nineties was still a very different place. We were coming out of a fair bit of turmoil, but still at that stage when there simply wasn't much to do.

'We didn't do much to make things more appealing for the new fans, it was just a few bells and whistles really. Face painting, singers, the Guinness vans, but it all built into that Friday feeling and we'd had some great nights.'

Becoming another famous victim – the latest would-be conqueror to be vanquished by the hometown favourite – appealed little to Stade Français, and if Reid's innovations at the club to date were a huge reason for the French's reticence to play Ulster at Ravenhill on a Friday night, it would require plenty more thought from the organisation's figurehead to ensure the game took place in Belfast at all. In no small part due to the furore created by the French visitors, eleven thousand tickets had already been sold for a Friday-night fixture when in late December 1998 the game was moved, first to a Saturday evening and then to early afternoon. Regardless of the when, the how was still a concern when it came to ensuring the ground would be approved by health and safety. It was little wonder that the CEO pondered whether Christmas in the Reid household might just have to wait until January.

There was no problem with demand for tickets, Rab Irwin could attest to that. The former builder had been asked to put his skills to good use, all for the promise of a few extra pounds on his pay cheque, after high winds in a new-year storm damaged the stadium gates. Indeed, he would have been deployed to fix the holes in the roof over the main stand, too, if not for the decision that a key player that high up a ladder was a bad idea. As Irwin worked away at the repairs, he saw queues of people waiting in line to secure their place in the ground. As one fan clutching a pair of tickets walked past, he gave away his lack of familiarity with the team he was paying to see.

'Jeez, for all the work you're doing up there I hope they're giving you some free tickets,' he shouted up to Irwin, who minutes later hopped down from his ladder to get ready for the morning's training session.

For Reid, it seemed that when one hurdle was overcome, another appeared. Like when eight hundred temporary seats were installed along the touchline to inch capacity ever closer to the magic number of twenty thousand, and it was discovered that the changed layout meant advertising hoardings were now several metres short of covering the perimeter. Each time a problem arose, though, the band of staff, tradesmen and volunteers battled through. The only obstacle that ever felt insurmountable, however, came about because of the forecast of a heavy frost overnight. With kick-off now in the early afternoon, there would be treacherous conditions for fans making their way to the game, even if the pitch had thawed in time for a lunchtime inspection. Genuine fears of a postponement emerged. As key staff gathered to decide upon the best course of action, John Callaghan remembered his conversation with Mo Mowlam the previous week. 'If you need anything at all, just ask,' the secretary of state had said to the Ulster president. A throwaway remark this may have been but Mowlam, or at the very least her office, was true to her word. After groundsman Bob Montgomery put in a call, and despite minor matters like ensuring the peace process could survive the instability caused by the ongoing disputes over decommissioning, Stormont quickly had gritting lorries circling BT6. Whatever the weather threw at the stadium between then and kick-off, Ulster were braced.

As evening gave way to night, Mike Reid sat alone in the stand surveying the remarkable transformation of the stadium. He had one last decision to make: floodlights. With so many of Ulster's memorable victories coming under the glare of the megawatt bulbs, Reid thought it foolish to change a winning formula. So, at a cost of seven hundred pounds and utterly unnecessarily given the kick-off time, the lights were to be left on until the game was over. If Stade didn't want to come to Belfast at night, Ulster would bring night to them.

Driving home, Reid pulled over to allow himself one last, lingering look at Ravenhill. Resplendent under the lights, the stadium was as ready as it ever could be.

The next day, the final tally that could safely filter through Rab Irwin's recently repaired gates and into the ground stood at 19,602 … some 398 short of the magic number. Thankfully, what with so much terracing, the French couldn't carry out their threat to count each paying customer on the way in, and what the European officials didn't know wouldn't hurt them. All that was left for Reid to do was to see how things played out on the field – if only he could. Having been delayed getting to the box thanks to some last-minute money counting, there wasn't a spare seat in the house, not one facing the action anyway. Instead he watched the opening exchanges on a black-and-white television under the stand.

17
THE TRY

Publicly, Stade Français were unfazed by Toulouse's exit at the hands of Ulster. With typical French candour, they told the media that their French rivals, previously thought to be the only side who could stop them winning their first European crown, had not been playing well regardless, especially away from home, and that they had anticipated the unfancied and unfashionable Irish side's advance to the last four.

Privately, they knew that if there was one lesson to take from the game that saw their countrymen come a cropper, it was the need to prepare for Belfast's typical weather conditions. Playing in Ravenhill it was almost expected that the rain would pour from the heavens and the hosts would hoist the ball skywards to meet it halfway. The northern province were seen as a wet-weather team, for in truth what choice did they have? As Toulouse had found to their cost, some torrential rain or swirling winds would do little to deter Simon Mason off the tee, and if the opposition weren't prepared for the conditions, no matter the stars they had on show, their visit would be uncomfortable.

Not prepared to suffer the same fate as Toulouse, Stade had spent the two weeks prior to the semi-final training in the Bois de Boulogne, a two thousand-acre public park along the western edge of the sixteenth arrondissement of Paris. It was a stone's throw from their Stade Jean-Bouin home and was nicknamed 'The Swamp' by Stade's players. Toiling away in the muck and the mire would be perfect preparation for their upcoming trip – or so they figured.

'I opened my windows on the morning of a game always hoping that it was wet and windy because the opposition wouldn't like it,' says David Humphreys. 'The morning of the semi-final, when the forecast had been for rain all week, I woke up and looked out to see the sun shining bright, a perfect winter's day.'

Despite their arduous preparation, there was little doubt among those heading to Ravenhill that the unexpectedly benign conditions would be a welcome relief to Stade, a side who liked to play expansive rugby, especially now their diminutive Italian playmaker Diego Dominguez was restored to the ten jersey. If Stade were concerned by the talents of the opposition, they were hardly showing it.

Ulster's own preparations had been somewhat harrowing, quite apart from the nervous rush to get their stadium up to scratch. For most of the two-week lead-up to the game, it seemed a given that Mark McCall would make his long-hoped-for comeback. The club captain hadn't hit a tackle bag in anger for four months but had been named to start in Dungannon's first All-Ireland League game of 1999 against DLSP a week before the last-four tie. His timely return was much to the delight of his club coach Willie Anderson, whose battle for promotion to the top tier of the All-Ireland League had been fought largely without his big-name professional recruits. With the side looking to bounce back from a surprising defeat to Portadown just before Christmas, McCall was to be in the twelve jersey. But when the Stevenson Park outfit took to the field on 2 January, the Irish international was absent; flu was given as the reason for his non-appearance. With the illness seen as minor in comparison to the serious neck problem he appeared to have overcome, hope remained that he'd make his long-awaited return on the biggest of stages.

'I feel fit and well, despite the long break, and would love to be picked,' McCall told the media just days before Harry Williams was due to name his team. 'In normal circumstances, had Stanley McDowell and van Rensburg been available, it would probably have made more sense to have me in the substitutes but now I'm not sure what's going to happen. If Harry Williams believes that I'm capable of doing a job and picks me to start that would be great. I know the system and have been training hard in recent weeks. My difficulty is a lack of match practice. It would have been great to have returned for Dungannon last Saturday but unfortunately I had a touch of flu and there was no point in risking things. But that has gone now and I've trained with Ulster this week. Basically, I've made myself available and it's up to Harry Williams.'

It was understandable why Ulster were so desperate to have him, especially with Stan McDowell still injured. Fresh pleas to have Clinton van Rensburg, the South African who last featured against Edinburgh, released fell on deaf ears. Rather than the cup semi-final in front of a packed-to-the-rafters Ravenhill, van Rensburg was told he'd bench behind Scott Gibbs and Mark Taylor against Cardiff in a friendly game designed solely to ward off any developing cobwebs.

McCall trained with the team right up until the side was announced in a special press conference on the Thursday afternoon, forty-eight hours before the game. All coach and player had been waiting for was an insurance company agreeing to cover the player. None would. A devastating blow, but one that was soon put into perspective. Despite the huge strides he'd made in his recovery, McCall was walking through town with his wife Kerry, only weeks after he had declared himself fit to take on Stade Français, when a passer-by bumped into him. At walking pace the impact hardly seemed serious, but McCall's back went into spasm for two days – the range of motion in his neck reduced pretty much to zero. The threat of sustaining a more lasting or even permanent injury from a heavy collision on a rugby field simply wasn't worth the risk. Ulster's captain had played his last game of rugby.

And while the team were outwardly playing it cool, on the eve of the game there remained the very real possibility that their talisman would miss out on the semi-final too. David Humphreys' shoulder had been the source of much consternation for Harry Williams ever since the Toulouse game.

'We were running out of backs by that point,' says Williams. 'Up front we had Gary Leslie, Stuarty Duncan, Ritchie Weir, Derick Topping, so an injury there we could have coped with, but it was last man standing almost in the backs. We didn't have much cover anyway but we'd already lost Mark McCall and Stan McDowell was out at that time too. Jan Cunningham was doing a good job moved into the centre, but we then had the two young boys on the wings. Jimmy Topping was out too, remember. It was the same at out-half. If Humphreys was out, it would have been a huge loss. Bryn Cunningham would have come in, only a young fella then, but I don't even know who would have been on the bench.'

Thankfully it didn't come to pass. Despite requiring a painkilling injection and substantial padding before taking the field, Humphreys began in his familiar ten jersey. It would prove one of his, and indeed Ulster Rugby's, most memorable days.

If few would have predicted it looking at the teams, anyone dreaming of an Ulster win would likely have had their hopes crushed had they been witness to Ulster's final training session before the biggest game of their lives. It was, to put it politely, an unmitigated disaster.

'I still come back to that session even now, even at schoolboy level, as an example of what it can mean when you have one of those team runs,' muses Simon Mason. 'It was without doubt the worst team run I've ever been involved in in my entire life. We couldn't train at Ravenhill. We were in the school just behind the stadium, and we couldn't pass the ball from one person to the next. We couldn't win a line-out. People were nearly in tears. I think that was when the nerves started to get to people.

'I remember afterwards thinking as long as we compete with them, we'll be all right. I had all this family over from England, all staying in the Welly Park Hotel and by the time the game was here, there was a part of you thinking as long as we don't get battered, it'll be an all right day.'

It was a day that began at an ungodly hour, thanks to the early kick-off. Harry Williams had his players assemble at the Wellington Park Hotel – a drop goal's distance from their favourite watering hole, The Bot, at ten in the morning. In the days prior to the game, the coach had been making some early forays into video analysis using a recently bought computer. He watched every video tape he could get his hands on of Stade playing, and logged what type of attack they launched and from where in each of their domestic games. Somewhat surprisingly for a side with such an array of talent, he came to the conclusion that they were in fact quite predictable opposition. Through the use of a flip chart, he outlined this to his players as they sat in the lobby before they left for the stadium. As he came to the last page he said, 'And this is what awaits you if you win,' before flipping over the sheet to reveal a crudely drawn bag with dollar signs on it. Once again, he'd broken the tension.

The fans had begun arriving at half eleven in the morning – the early start had done little to dampen their spirits and, in the words of David Humphreys, there was 'electricity' in the air come kick-off. The first six points of the game came from Mason's boot – the very same man who had earlier hoped his side at least wouldn't embarrass themselves until the welcoming roar from the stands convinced him that this was to be their day. He scored a penalty and an audacious snap drop goal off a missed touch-finder from Dominguez. And it wasn't long after the ball curled inside the far upright that Allen Clarke stood on the sideline, ball in hand, waiting to deliver into the line-out. The hooker, with the crowd in the temporary seats practically within touching distance and willing his dart to find its mark, took a long deep breath as he dried the ball with a vigour that seemed likely to take the leather off.

The set piece can be a funny thing for a man wearing a number two on his back. The line-out requires many men doing many jobs, but it's one of life's certainties that should it go wrong the hooker throwing the ball in is the one who takes all the flak. Hours and hours for years and years go into practising the art, designed so that in pressured moments, such as these, muscle memory kicks in and limits the risk of what could be a game defining miscue. There was no mistake this time as Clarke stretched back and fired into the throng of bodies. Gary Longwell reached up to claim the dart, and as the Ulster forwards swarmed around him the ball was filtered back down the chain and, in a move of beautiful simplicity, there was no stopping the drive that ended with Stephen McKinty touching down.

The scrum was the only area in which Stade Français had the upper hand. 'That Marconnet … a rhinoceros of a prop,' remembers Rab Irwin, still with some wonderment in his voice. After those quick-fire eleven points, Ulster didn't score again for the remainder of the first-half. Thankfully Stade, the supposed free-flowing and free-scoring superstars, weren't clicking. There was little incision, but one instance of blunt trauma when Christophe Juillet matched McKinty's maul try. Dominguez, so used to being the conductor of the orchestra, found himself in the unfamiliar position of playing second fiddle, but still converted the score which, in addition to an earlier penalty, left his side just one point in arrears at the break.

Just after the restart: history – largely accidental history. After gathering from the base of a retreating scrum, number nine Andy Matchett, building upon his composed showing against Toulouse, fired a strong flat pass into David Humphreys. The expectation was that the out-half would offer the first serve in a game of kick tennis: fire the ball long in the hope that, at the very best, he'd find a patch of grass and gain an edge in the territory battle. The beauty of Humphreys, of course, was that he didn't always deal in the expected. Instead of looking for distance or the sideline, the out-half chipped delicately forward, finding not just space but space in an area where his side would be able to regather the ball.

'I didn't really see it,' says Williams. 'I had my head in my hands. I was sat where I could see all the space up the sideline where he should have booted it. What do coaches know, eh?'

Contrary to popular belief, the move was neither improvised nor perfectly executed. Humphreys' kick fell into the arms of Sheldon Coulter who, running furiously after taking the catch, suddenly found that there was only Sebastien Viars, and some half of the field, between himself and the try line.

'David and I were having a conversation before the scrum,' says the winger. 'The original plan was just to take the pass and put the ball as deep into the stand as it would go. But we were stood there and the more we talked it through, the more we just thought "Listen, let's play it and see what happens."

'He was supposed to kick it, catch it, pass it to me and I'd be away. It turned out to be opposite as when the chip went up I thought I had the best chance of taking it. Lucky enough it worked out.'

Coulter worked what had developed into the two on one expertly, drawing the French full back and giving the ball back to Humphreys in the clear. As Humphreys disappeared into the distance, the only man giving realistic chase was flanker Christophe Moni. When the mismatched loose forward dropped his hands and gave up the chase, Ravenhill erupted.

The television gantry, attached to the far stand, shook with the force of the celebrations. The 52 per cent of Northern Ireland's television-watching public who were glued to their screens saw Humphreys dive across the whitewash as if they were watching clothes being thrown around a washing machine on spin cycle.

From the out-half coming on to the ball, just seven seconds had elapsed before he was diving to down the ball, arguably the most memorable handful of clock ticks the stadium had witnessed since Ireland won their Grand Slam there in 1948. So many were swept up in the euphoria of Ulster's run and coming to the old ground for the first time, little did they know that they likely wouldn't see a better or more important score no matter how many more times they stood shoulder to shoulder on the terraces. Ever the marketing man, Mike Reid smiled to himself when he realised that what was to become something of an immortalised image featured the captain diving right in front of the hoarding with the Bank of Ireland logo, coincidentally his chief sponsor. Advertising that money can't buy. The slogan 'Doesn't half-back business' was soon attached and a campaign that appeared across the country in the coming weeks was born.

'It was the most memorable try I ever scored,' says Humphreys. 'All I had to do was run, but when you think about it in the context of that game, in the context of the competition, that was the first time that people really started to think about Ravenhill as this tough place to go and play. The crowd was electric.

'I'd done no training in the build-up, I played that whole game on adrenaline. Of all the games I played across twenty-odd years of rugby, that day will always be the highlight. They were the best team in Europe and we outplayed them.'

As Ravenhill digested the majesty of what it had just witnessed, Mason converted and added another penalty before Humphreys got on the scoresheet again. If his try was a thing of beauty, his drop goal was the ugly duckling of the season. A shaky trajectory right off the boot, the ball's flight through the air was described as being akin to that of a 'drunken torpedo' by BBC NI commentator Jim Neilly. The net result was the same, though – three points to Ulster. They led 24–10.

With the maul Stade's most effective way of forcing a breakthrough, and Ulster still giving away too many penalties, the opposing pack rumbled over for another with Juillet again the man providing the finish, but Mason, and what had assuredly become the most famous right boot in Ulster, kept them at arm's length with two more penalties.

French international Marc Livermont, who had been forced to make do with a place on the bench to start the contest, grabbed an almost identical mauled score to Stade's first to once again cut the deficit, this time to only three points, and, as with the game against Toulouse, the final minutes were spent wondering if this was going to be another of Ulster's valiant defeats: the most memorable of journeys seemed to be running out of steam with the finishing line in sight.

Once more, though, this Ulster team proved to be of a different stock as the only score in the final throes came off the tee from Mason. It was a central penalty but one from just inside the opposition half that still required every ounce of his expertise. When the final whistle sounded, the Liverpudlian, who had long since gained honorary Ulsterman status, was corralled by a sideline television reporter for a snap interview. As the microphone was thrust towards him, fans hopped over the hoardings and streamed both towards and past him.

With the seventeen men who had bested the most fancied team in Europe joined by thousands of supporters, some old, some new, Harry Williams ambled down onto the sod. A crumpled Stade Français flag with a broken pole lay discarded on the turf. A nice souvenir of the biggest day of his coaching career, he thought. Sadly, in a packed changing room – even First Minister David Trimble was in there congratulating everyone on their seismic achievement (including one slightly bemused local newspaper reporter) – the memento disappeared, never to be seen again.

When the players eventually left the stadium, making their way back to the Wellington Park, the scoreboard by the memorial clock still read Ulster 33–27 Stade Français. It stayed that way for more than a month. Nobody was yet ready or willing to destroy any shred of evidence that confirmed what had just happened.

18
SUPERSTARS

Sport has a way of bringing you back down to earth with something of a bump. Days after the Stade Français game, national coach Warren Gatland announced his squad for a Galway training camp to prepare for the upcoming Five Nations. The championship's first game was against France in Lansdowne Road, just seven days after the European Cup final that, thanks to Ulster's success, would now be in the same venue. Twenty-six men were called up with a further two youngsters invited to sample the environment – what, one wonders, ever happened to Brian O'Driscoll and Gordon D'Arcy? The usual Ulster suspects were there: David Humphreys, Justin Fitzpatrick, Jonny Bell and Andy Ward – so too exiles Jeremy Davidson and Paddy Johns and the displaced Leinster native Eric Miller. Absent, however, was Simon Mason – the face, and boot, behind what was Irish Rugby's most successful European campaign to date. It was suspected that the full back would be called up at the very least to offer cover for Conor O'Shea. Gatland, however, stuck with Leinster and Terenure's Girvan Dempsey.

'In the area of defence, I still believe he has a weakness,' the coach told the press, not ruling out that he could add to his three caps at a later point in the campaign.

This was just the situation when Harry Williams came into his own. Players, like pupils back when he was a teacher, all required a different approach and, while the likes of Gary Longwell, himself unfortunate to miss out, could be fired up by a snub like a bear that had been poked, his goalkicker required more of a comforting arm around the shoulder.

'Harry found the way to keep everyone in this amazingly positive mindset,' recalls Mason. 'He really was so underestimated. He was this wily sort of football-type manager and he was old school in his values. After Ireland stuff or whatever, he brought me in and just told me I was the first person on his team sheet every week. Now, we had far better players than me – Andy Ward, David Humphreys, Jonny Bell, so he won't have meant it, but he just gave me that positivity. We never talked about the work ons, any missed tackles or that, it was always just positive reinforcement. He always left you thinking, "I'm just part of a jigsaw that Harry Williams has put together." He never made you feel like you had to do anything that wasn't your game, it wasn't like he'd ever expect me to counter from the twenty-two or anything.'

Regardless of who Gatland selected, it wasn't a winter that promised much for the national side – they would ultimately win one game which was, at least, one better than the year before – and, as such, interest in Ulster's run was even greater. There were three weeks between the vanquishing of Stade and taking on Colomiers – three weeks for the already mushrooming support to grow even more.

Suddenly, the most sought-after fashion item in Belfast was an Ulster jersey, with stockists SS Moore describing the rush as akin to a second Christmas. Two thousand were sold and when more hit the shelves they were snapped up within hours. Usually taking six weeks to come in from Canterbury, a rush had to be put on the next shipments to meet demand ahead of the final. However, what no fans could get their hands on was the jersey Ulster would actually be wearing at Lansdowne Road. In the days before away, alternate and even European jerseys were commonplace, Ulster found themselves having to switch to red thanks to a colour clash with Colomiers. Only twenty-five of the new strip were ever made – all guarded like a hawk by the side's beloved bag man Willie Wallace – and the always meticulous Williams had his side train in the colours to avoid any shock to the system come match day.

Indeed, the only thing scarcer than jerseys proved to be tickets – demand exceeding supply by two to one. With an initial allocation of nineteen thousand – that it was always hoped would be boosted by returns from Colomiers who planned on bringing a maximum of a few thousand – there was simply no way to ensure tickets went to the most deserving. With the farthest reaches of the province more than a four-hour round trip from Belfast, it was felt that first come, first served was unfair, and so tickets were allocated via a ballot, but even that didn't stop some fans queuing with their application forms from the early hours in a line that snaked out of the ground and down the surrounding streets.

It was a case of all hands on deck, with players taking turns in the office to stuff and lick envelopes. While there was no option but to use the squad for this work, how successfully they turned their hand to administrative work was called into question when a fan who was unfortunate enough not to secure the fifty pounds worth of tickets he had applied for was sent a refund with an extra hundred pounds. When he called the office to enquire as to how to return the surplus funds, he unsurprisingly found the phone line permanently engaged.

While the crowd at the Stade Français game had been their biggest for decades, the final was a different beast all together. With only one ticket window serving the thousands trying to make their application, there simply wasn't the infrastructure to cope. Added to that, team manager John Kinnear was trying to run crowd control armed with only a loudspeaker. Most understood the efforts being made in unprecedented circumstances, but the frustrations of a few boiled over. One fan confronted CEO Mike Reid to let him know what he thought of the organisation.

'This is a disgrace,' said the disgruntled customer. 'I've wasted three hours of my day.'

'Three hours?' replied Reid, naturally concerned at the annoyance of any long-term supporter.

'Aye,' replied the offended party. 'Two hours in the queue, and it took me an hour finding the bloody stadium in the first place.'

The righteous indignation of the odd blow-in or two was an unavoidable consequence, but there was genuine concern that the increased attention on the side would leave those who had been familiar faces on the terraces for years without a way to see this most eagerly anticipated contest.

'The media profile just exploded and it gave everyone this sense that no matter what happened they had to be there,' remembers Reid. 'We had three or four journalists who were usually at everything, but during that season it just went bananas. We had press conferences for two weeks with ten or eleven television cameras surrounding the players whenever they spoke. It was unheard of.

'The hard part was the IRFU weren't used to it either. It was before Ticketmaster and things like that, so manually was the only option. We wouldn't do it the same way now, but that's the way it was then. We had five of us in that office, a couple of part-timers, but we had to get the players in … literally rows of them sitting there putting tickets in envelopes and Masey answering the phones.

'Everyone felt they had to be at that game. I remember seeing my aunt and uncle there, fully decked out in the red and white Ulster wigs. They hadn't been to an Ulster game before in their lives. There was a real worry at the start but we just kept getting more tickets dropped to us. In the end, I've never met anyone who wanted a ticket who couldn't get one. Ulster people will always find a way.'

Still, after the sold-out signs went up at Ravenhill, BBC NI took advantage of the hysteria in their advertising campaign, running pictures of a sprinting David Humphreys along with the slogan, 'Millions of seats still available'.

Whenever players weren't manning positions in the ticket office, Harry Williams was insistent that the three weeks between the semi-final and final were kept as close to routine as possible. While it would be a wholly anachronistic notion just a few short years later, first that meant turning out for their club sides in the All-Ireland League.

Dungannon could hardly have faced a longer trip, travelling all the way to Cork to face Sunday's Well, but it was worth it as a try from the fit-again Stephen Bell and eight points from the boot of Humphreys contributed to an 18–11 win. Ballymena's large Ulster contingent faced a similarly arduous journey to Galwegians only to see their game called off due to adverse weather on the west coast.

Showing an early aptitude for somewhat unconventional, yet undeniably effective, man-management, Mark McCall was heavily relied upon by Williams at this time. Having never allowed his own circumstances to darken his mood, the club captain was every inch the future coach as he went round the squad doing his utmost to ensure the size of the looming occasion was not weighing too heavily upon anyone's shoulders. 'Do what you normally would do,' he told the players. That meant several of the Dungannon set, along with Mason and a few others, out in Belfast a week before the final. 'Don't go necking vodka or anything but just do what you normally would, a few beers,' remembers Mason of the casual attitude back then. All well and good until one barman refused to serve them for fear of hindering their chances of being crowned European champions.

No matter how hard they tried, whether it be casual pints or their usual lunches on the Lisburn Road, the idea that the final was just another game could only last so long. Eventually interest in the game reached fever pitch – no matter where you went, it was the primary topic of conversation.

'I remember getting recognised in the street for the first time and it being the most bizarre thing,' recalls Andy Matchett, who by that stage had been representing Ulster for a decade. 'It was across the board. There was a cross-community aspect and everyone was backing us. It really was great but from our perspective as players you would have liked to be more focused on just the game. Everybody got caught up to a degree, in terms of requests for tickets and stuff like that.'

'It did go a bit silly,' admits Mason. 'For two weeks it was just what it's like being a professional footballer. I just wanted to go kick and there I was having photo shoots with people taking pictures of my feet. It wasn't people being overbearing or anything, but it did become consuming. It was all positive but it was like grannies coming up and shaking your hand in the post office and telling you that you better win.'

In an effort to extricate the players from the furore and hype, Williams took the decision to bring his side to Dublin two days early, on Thursday afternoon. The squad assembled at Central Station for the twelve thirty Enterprise service to Dublin. They were in good spirits, spectacularly kitted out in garish tracksuits that were a heady mix of colours that had no business being on the same garment. On the rare occasion the squad of the 1980s went on tour, they did so wearing second-hand Nottingham Forest gear with an Ulster badge stitched over the crest. Any pangs of jealousy that squad felt over the greater choice and number of freebies on offer since their day were no doubt dispelled at the sight of those outfits.

'It was awful,' says Mark Blair. 'At the time we thought it was great, but then you look at photos and wonder how somebody got paid to design that.'

Unsurprisingly, given their just-the-same-as-any-other-week mantra, the journey to Dublin was spent with various card games running, while Stuart Duncan and Andy Ward walked the carriage with the intention of winding up any willing, or unwilling, victim. Arriving into Dublin's Connolly Station by mid-afternoon, the squad were in the southern capital before the mass exodus from Belfast commenced, and could make their way to the Berkeley Court Hotel, less than a ten-minute stroll from Lansdowne Road, unhindered. As the players collected their bags and prepared to check in, they weren't quite anonymous but they weren't far off. When one passing fan stopped to get Andy Ward's autograph, the Kiwi informed him that he was leaving without the signature of his fellow flanker Stephen McKinty who stood beside them.

With the game still forty-eight hours away, there was plenty of time to kill, which proved something of a challenge for the two youngest members of the squad, close friends Sheldon Coulter and Andy Park. The pair had known each other since they were both fighting for the same out-half spot on an Ulster underage team, meeting when on opposing sides in a probables versus possibles trial, and now they sat on the cusp of the biggest game of their lives, both transformed into wingers.

For the first time, the pair were rooming together, which proved to be both a blessing and a curse. While their more experienced teammates travelled with plenty of books, newspapers and the customary decks of cards, Park and Coulter were brimming with nervous energy. The odd game of corridor cricket provided something of a release, but they were aghast when told that a walk into the city centre wasn't advised for fear it would take too much out of their legs.

'There's only so much banter you can have when you're there for two days,' says Park. 'No phones in those days or anything. Me and Shelly were warned, "Don't get yourselves too excited so you can't sleep," like a couple of kids. It was a bit claustrophobic. The Irish internationals were more used to it, they'd done it before, right down to being in the same hotel, but it wasn't for me. You were hanging around doing nothing – ultimately you were on your arse all day.

'You just had to find a way to keep the banter going. If you were a team of all quiet guys, it'd be pretty boring. Me and Shelly were a bit more jubilant in those days, I suppose. It changes when you get older – you've more stress on your shoulders. We knew when to be serious, when to switch on, but we enjoyed it too. Not everyone can be like that. Gary Longwell used to say there's nobody he'd like to be stuck in a lift with less than me. I'd probably say the same about him. Even for me, there's only so much talking I can do when someone isn't talking back.'

One unique way to pass the time on this particular occasion was to read through the flood of faxes being sent to the Berkeley Court. So numerous were the messages that Harry Williams had them covering the walls of the team room. From all corners of the country, and all walks of life, they left the team sure that they were now representing far more than merely Ulster's rugby fraternity. GAA clubs far and wide offered their support; so too the other provinces.

'I'd say it choked some of them boys from the likes of Munster and Leinster having to sign them,' laughs Williams.

There was even one sent to captain David Humphreys from the prime minister. In a handwritten note sent from a hotel in Vienna, Tony Blair said:

> Dear David, what an amazing job to get into the final. Well done – the whole country is behind you! Best wishes and good luck to all the players.

Despite everything they'd experienced in the build-up, come the eve of the match the players still weren't sure what to expect from the next day. They struggled to comprehend the sheer numbers from the province who would make the journey south come the morning of the game. It was only when some gathered in the team room to watch *Kelly* – a local talk show broadcast on UTV which, in Northern Ireland at least, attracted three times as many viewers as BBC institution *Parkinson* – that they got some idea of the numbers leaving Belfast. The *Belfast Telegraph* dubbed the game 'The people's final' after it was estimated that six thousand cars were making the journey down the M1 with another ten thousand fans being ferried by Ulsterbus. One travel company even investigated the possibility of hiring the high-speed catamaran SeaCat, usually reserved for Belfast to Scotland crossings, to make the journey to Dublin.

By the time the players woke on the morning of the game, the streets were heaving with red-and-white-clad followers. While the old phrase 'Last one out turn off the lights' didn't quite apply, it certainly seemed that anyone who had ever tripped over a rugby ball had decamped to Dublin, with one friend telling Murtagh Rea it was as if the Twelfth of July was being held on Grafton Street. Among the travellers were some key figures of the peace process: First Minister David Trimble and his deputy Seamus Mallon were to be in the crowd, so too Secretary of State Mo Mowlam, the Irish Taoiseach Bertie Ahern and the president of Ireland, Belfast-born Mary McAleese. While not there in an official capacity, also due to attend was Sinn Féin leader Gerry Adams, who had watched Ulster for the very first time on television during the semi-final, although he'd previously witnessed South Africa play France during the 1995 World Cup when invited as a guest of the ANC. There were times in years gone by when getting these men and women in the same room at the same time had seemed an impossible task, even with the very future of the province at stake, yet all for the sake of eighty minutes of rugby, here they were united behind the same cause.

With the squad converging on Park's and Coulter's room,

from where they could see the streets surrounding the hotel from the window, the number of their supporters finally became clear.

'We were on the top floor looking out the window and there was a mass of red and white,' says Williams. 'All down Haddington Road, everywhere you looked, there wasn't a blade of grass or a spot of concrete to be seen, it was just a mass of bodies.'

With the windows of the breakfast room opened after the morning team meeting, the cheers and merriment from outside drifted through the hotel as the players ate, and Colin Wilkinson buzzed from table to table telling the players of the unprecedented accuracy displayed by Simon Mason in his morning kicking session. With their bus waiting outside, when the players made their way through the lobby, marching single file through a wall of noise created by a couple of hundred fans, friends and family members, emotions began to swell.

'Walking down those steps, walking into the foyer, you felt that sense of pride in where you're from,' says Allen Clarke, who woke at the crack of dawn on the morning of the final and walked the streets of Dublin to gather his thoughts. 'There was definitely a tear in the eye. You could taste the atmosphere. Where we're from, what Ulster, what Northern Ireland and what Ireland had been going through, you recognised there was an expectation for something special to happen. It didn't feel like a weight on the shoulders, it was like an energy in the body. It made me feel as if I could have run all day. In my head, we were never going to lose that game.'

Clarke wasn't the only one of Ulster's hardy forwards moved to tears by the scene. Gary Longwell, the lock who a few years after the European campaign asked an Ireland team doctor to amputate a broken finger solely so he could play a Six Nations game, had been overcome all week, and was only calmed the night before by a reassuring talk from David Humphreys.

As the bus pulled out of the Berkeley Court, the driver headed left instead of right, and transformed a journey that should have only taken a couple of minutes into one that took the side right around the block. The trip took considerably longer than planned but gave the squad an opportunity to soak up yet more of the occasion. When the bus stopped at the traffic lights outside the Beggars Bush pub, fans enjoying early-morning refreshments piled around either side of the coach, banging on the windows and shouting encouragement from the very bottom of their lungs. As the lights turned green, and for the remainder of the journey to the ground, the throng of well-wishers parted like the Red Sea to allow the men of the hour through. It was part of the day ingrained in the minds of many players, all who thought it was a master stroke by Williams to amp the players up one final time.

'Oh, no, it was nothing to do with me,' the coach admits. 'I don't know why the bus driver did it. Instead of turning right and going down the wee road straight to Lansdowne he went left and did a lap round. I think he thought it was an easier way to get where he needed parked. When the bus stopped outside the Beggars Bush it was very emotional, and it's been well-documented now but I was swearing under my breath at the driver.'

Having arrived at the stadium, there were more tears as McCall walked round the dressing room, wishing luck to those about to take the field. Coulter was absent – in the bathroom vomiting. Having done the same before the wins over Toulouse and Stade Français, he considered it a positive omen. On such days, every little helps.

19
BLOOD BROTHERS

Stuart Duncan was a large lump of a man. If he were to run head first into a wall, your first reaction would be to check the brickwork for damage.

On the morning of the European final, it was approaching a decade since his Ulster debut – which had been a run-out against Yorkshire in 1989 as a nineteen-year-old. His first visit to Lansdowne Road, where Ulster and Colomiers would do battle for European rugby's biggest prize, had come years before that when he made the journey to Dublin with his family to see big brother Willie make his debut for Ireland. A visiting Wales side won 16–9 that February afternoon in 1984, but nonetheless the members of the Duncan household were proud to see their son ousting the famed Fergus Slattery from the side and pulling on a green jersey for a first time.

Stuart was fourteen then, thirteen years younger than his elder sibling, and despite the international pedigree of his brother, Stuart's rugby experience to that point had been minimal. He had attended Orangefield High, the East Belfast school that counted singer Van Morrison among its notable alumni, where rugby was far from prominent. It was for that very reason that Bryce Fleming saw an opportunity. Fleming had been rugby development officer at Malone RFC before such a position ever truly existed, and would stand at the fence of Gibson Park, on the little through road known locally as Daddy Winker's Lane, and challenge passers-by, usually pupils from Grosvenor or Orangefield taking a shortcut to school, to use rugby to prove they really were as tough as they thought. It was a tactic that worked wonders for the club, which was able to field multiple under-eighteen sides when most youngsters of that age played rugby in school or not at all.

Stuart was one of his early protégés and was soon captivated by the sport, honing his skills at Malone while taking every opportunity to watch his brother in action for Ulster. When the side of 1984 were preparing to take on the fearsome Wallabies, a side that would beat Ireland, England, Scotland and Wales, but not Ulster, it was he who was stood on the sidelines and retrieved the ball for Jimmy Davidson if it ever, God forbid, squirted out of the scrum where the likes of JJ McCoy, Stevie Smith and John McDonald were doing battle.

Soon enough, though, he was not just Willie's brother: he was making an impact of his own. When Ulster under-eighteen selectors turned up to one underage game to run the rule over Malone's number eight, the wrong jerseys had been handed out and the impressive boy they thought they were there to see was not in fact the intended target of their scouting mission but Stuart Duncan, a fifteen-year-old with three seasons of eligibility still left at that level.

By the time the 1995 European Cup began for Ulster with a trip to Cardiff, Duncan had established himself in the starting side. He filled the same wing forward role once held by his older brother for the side's first European win over Caledonia when David Humphreys accounted for twenty-three points in the high-scoring 34–41 away triumph. Despite changing coaches and captains, he'd been ever-present over the course of those first two seasons of the Heineken Cup, but a serious knee injury left him a peripheral figure over the next twenty-four months. By the time he'd battled back to fitness, Andy Ward had debuted and Tony McWhirter transformed from a lock into a number eight. With Stephen McKinty a most trusted lieutenant of his fellow Bangor man Harry Williams, the Ward-McWhirter-McKinty trio had been the first choice throughout the entire 1998–99 campaign. But that didn't stop Duncan hoping to change the coach's mind.

As the final approached, he was the last Malone man standing, a host of his fellow clubmen, including his good friend Murtagh Rea, having fallen by the wayside since the squad first assembled in August. He'd been an unused substitute against Stade Français, as well as in the win over Toulouse in pool stages, but otherwise had been a replacement in each European tie. Indeed, if not for his late intervention in shutting down a three-on-one overlap in the latter stages against Edinburgh in the opening game, one match point could have been none, the quarter-final with Toulouse subsequently on the road rather than in Ravenhill. In a season where so many small moments combined to create the perfect storm, Duncan had provided one of his own in the very first game.

Starting or not, Duncan was a valuable member of the panel – one of the archetypal good squad men who were so vital in engendering the camaraderie that had developed in the group. Aside from a quick wit and a penchant for storytelling, his proficiency at board games was the stuff of legend, especially for former coach Tony Russ who, before a past European tussle with Harlequins, had told the squad to decimate the opposition in the way that Duncan had decimated him at chess the night before. It was Duncan who made the game of Risk so popular throughout the squad that during the season an A and B league had been set up – his own brand of back-room diplomacy often geared towards deals that would ensure David Humphreys didn't end the game victorious.

'Stuarty didn't get a lot of game time that year but he's a spiritual leader in many ways,' says Tony McWhirter. 'The Dunk was one of the guys at my first training session. I was nineteen and I was holding the bag for the first time and the first four boys through were Davy Tweed, Paddy Johns, Jeremy Davidson and Dunky. I got fucking smashed by all of them, but then Dunky was the first one over at the end of the session to tell you, "Well done, son," and give you a pat on the back. He's still like that. He's still a great guy. If you were doing something, good or bad, Stuarty was the first one there. For guys like me, he was a bit older at that stage, so when I first started paying attention to the Ulster senior team at fourteen or fifteen, he was there and synonymous with being a hardman. He'd quite happily knock someone's front teeth out for you if they had it coming. For me, I still have a good bond with him even now.'

On the morning of the European Cup final, Duncan knew just what the game meant to the people of Ulster: he'd seen the evidence first-hand. Driving a lorry for the plumbing supplies company Beggs and Partners, he was recognised by clients who had shown no interest in the sport before. Traversing the province, from Belfast out towards GAA heartlands, he was pumped for information on scrummaging positions or breakdown techniques by men who had previously only taken note of Gaelic football and hurling. Given that he had watched his brother when he was only a child, no player had been around Ulster longer, and none was more appreciative of how much had changed over the course of this magical run and how transformative one more victory could be. His would be the last voice the players would hear before they left the changing room for the field.

'If we win today, for the rest of our lives we'll be blood brothers,' he told them. 'Nobody can do it for us. We are the twenty-two players who can go out there and create history. When we meet up in years to come, we'll sit down and laugh and joke and remember this day as the one when we won the

European Cup. Go out there and become a legend.'

Plenty of fans were still milling about outside the stadium or in the concourses when the warm-ups began, even if there were already more than enough to make Colomiers aware that they weren't in friendly surroundings. David Humphreys and Mark McCall had visited Gloucester's Kingsholm stadium during their time in England. The way the fans of the cherry and whites had lifted the atmosphere when their players jogged around the perimeter of the pitch at the end of their warm-up had stayed with Humphreys and McCall.

'They hated going to Gloucester,' says McWhirter laughing. 'What Gloucester always did was that half lap around the pitch before they went in front of the Shed to get things fired up. They would tell you about that run around the Shed and you would imagine the fans throwing things at you, spitting at you. When they did that, you thought "Flip me, these boys are going to come out like cavemen here."'

Incorporating what he'd seen at Gloucester into his side's own preparations, Humphreys led the players around the touchline in what was to be one of their last acts before the biggest game in most of their lives. Like two cars in a game of chicken, it soon became clear that the teams were on a collision course. As Ulster circled around, Colomiers were running through some last-minute set-piece practice. Something, or someone, had to give. As Ulster neared, Marc dal Maso – the hooker, one of the French side's few internationals having joined from Agen the previous summer – stepped back as if he were preparing to throw the ball into an imaginary line-out. While the rest of the players went around him, Duncan was already in his game mindset and didn't want to give an inch.

He thought that to go around, to break his stride or alter his line, was a concession – something he was loath to do on a rugby field, whether the game had begun or not. The flanker barged through dal Maso with his shoulder, catching him unawares and knocking him sideways. When the Frenchman turned to find the culprit, he homed in on the wholly innocent Stanley McDowell, back on the bench after his hamstring injury at the expense of Robin Morrow.

'Maybe I brushed him a bit on the way past,' says Duncan, his diplomatic delivery failing to mask the mischievous glint in his eye.

'It got everyone into the game before it kicked off, even if it was only one or two percentage points,' adds McWhirter. 'They were probably looking round thinking, "What's going on?" Even when you think about just the decision to do that jog round, it's a testament to Mark and David. Where those guys ended up, the number of things like that that they thought of in the planning and the executing before things even kicked off, it's easy to see why they've done so well.'

If that got Ulster's blood pumping, what happened next only hardened their belief that this was to be a special day. With kick-off only moments away, the players stood and faced the East stand, where their fans were most concentrated, linked arms and then saluted the crowd. As they lifted their hands towards the crowd, Andy Park was nearly lifted off his feet. It felt as though the roared response from the crowd would lift the East stand's roof. The synergy between supporters and team was palpable. While individual sportsmen and women had acted as a unifying rather than a divisive force in Northern Ireland, a team that was truly representative of the troubled province was an almost unique phenomenon in the history of Northern Irish sport.

'It was the maddest warm-up,' says Andy Ward. 'I just remember thinking that we had to get this crowd pumping, I just knew that. Forty-odd thousand of them going mad, that would be the business. It got everyone jazzed up. Whenever we just ran right through them, Dunky dropping the shoulder, the crowd went off.

'Then the line, the salute, to do something like that as tight a bunch as we were, that just showed the crowd that we were all in it together. You could just see Colomiers thinking "What the hell are we in for here?" It felt like we had won that game before a ball was kicked. We were in the changing rooms and people just couldn't wait to get back out there and get it going. It was like an electric charge running through you or something.'

In the old Lansdowne Road, where the rattle and hum of the trains that ran underneath the West stand of the stadium could be both heard and felt during a game, the Orient Express could have been steaming across the twenty-two and had its engines drowned out by the roar.

Ulster, their twenty-two players and their tens of thousands of fans, were ready to go.

20
THE BLUEPRINT

Ulster's fairy-tale run to the final always had the feel of David taking on Goliath but Colomiers were no giants. A satellite of the city of Toulouse, the side were based in a town of just thirty thousand citizens and had spent their short existence in the shadow of their more illustrious next-door neighbours. The rugby club was only founded in 1963 and was part-owned by the town council, with beloved president Michel Bendichou having made his name as the owner of hardware stores. They had no silverware to boast of until, one year prior to their appearance in the showpiece final, they won the Europe Conference with a striking display of running rugby against Agen. Having also fallen just two wins short of claiming their first-ever Bouclier de Brennus, the small French side had certainly enjoyed their most memorable of campaigns.

Their 1998–99 season, though, had been markedly different despite their European run. Captain and local hero Jean-Luc Sadourny, the elegant full back who was one of the best fifteens of his generation, had missed almost all of the season with serious damage to his knee ligaments, returning to action only three weeks before the final. While he'd played in Dublin five times over the course of his international career, never losing to the Irish on their home patch, his recent injury troubles meant he hadn't been included in the French squad for the upcoming opening round of the 1999 Five Nations. His France teammate Fabien Galthié had endured a similarly disrupted campaign missing eight weeks with a broken wrist, during which time his side twice committed the cardinal sin of French rugby: losing at home, to both Grenoble and Brive. Galthié had lasted just forty-four minutes of his return match before injuring his thigh muscle. In the weeks building up to the final, Galthié, one of France's finest ever nines, berated himself for not taking more care to ensure he was sufficiently warmed up for the second half, blaming himself for the injury that threatened his participation in the final.

It all made for a season of marked contrasts. Domestically, the first month of 1999 brought a nervy 11–9 win over La Rochelle, a much-needed victory that staved off the embarrassment of failing to make it through to the last sixteen of the competition, but it came at a huge cost when integral lock Jean-Philippe Revallier dislocated an elbow, his hospital stay ruling him out of the trip to Dublin.

'We have not been able to live up to that status so far this season but we may have gotten over the worst,' said head coach Jacques Brunel of his side's domestic struggles ahead of the final. 'We will be better prepared to face Ulster because I have made the players understand it is their fault things have been going so badly. It is not the referee, it is not the opposing team, but themselves who are responsible for their own fate.'

It was, at least, a different story in Europe. Despite losing two games during the pool stages – both away, to Pontypridd and Glasgow – they still managed to land a home tie in the quarter-finals by virtue of winning pool four, even though best runners-up, Toulouse and Munster, boasted better tallies. It was the Irish side – whose own love affair with Europe was only a year away from kicking into high gear – that they beat in the last eight, running out on the right side of a comfortable 23–9 scoreline at the Stade Selery, but, like Ulster, they were given little hope of winning in the semi-finals. For Colomiers, the assignment was Perpignan, the Basque side who had finished runner-up to Stade Français in the French championship. Led by their inspirational captain, Thomas Lièvremont, the heavy favourites had been 6–3 ahead thanks to a pair of penalties from Benoît Bellot, but when Colomiers' nineteen-year-old wing, David Skrela, son of French selector Jean-Claude Skrela, charged down an attempted kick for a try and converted his own score, the deal was sealed. Colomiers were welcomed back to town by an army of fans wielding six hundred bags of blue and white confetti.

They had known the final would be a different challenge, especially having only beaten Treviso outside of France in the campaign. Even so, the media briefings during the week had seen both sides fight to bestow the tag of favourites upon the opposition, with David Humphreys' assertion that Ulster would always be the underdogs against French adversaries doing little to convince the public, or indeed Colomiers, that the more substantial hurdles had already been cleared in the shape of Toulouse and Stade.

'I fear that it is going to be even tougher than an international,' said Sadourny in the final presser. 'We have to admire the way Ulster have reached the final, they can feel very proud of what they achieved. But we also know that we will be playing against 16 players – 15 on the pitch and the collective noise of the crowd.'

With the eventful warm-up having whipped the crowd into a frenzy, Sadourny's prediction was correct as the match kicked off under a haze of smoke from the pyrotechnics. Stephen McKinty claimed the kick-off and made a beeline for an opposing back. Seeking an easy target, the flanker was given a rude awakening as he was taken low and almost lost possession. An inauspicious start but help, real or fanciful, was soon at hand in the form of his old raincoat. On the crisp winter afternoon Mark McCall had seen little need for the now lucky garment, tying it instead around his waist, but after Labit punished an Ulster offside with a thirty-metre penalty, he decided that regardless of the logic there was little point testing the fates on such an occasion. With the tattered windbreaker restored to its rightful place on McCall's torso, Ulster gained, if not quite seized, the upper hand; Mason's first penalty of the afternoon ensuring Colomiers lead lasted only four minutes. After a quarter of an hour the Liverpudlian, having now landed nearly forty straight kicks since beginning that morning on a deserted back pitch, gave Ulster the advantage, but, for all the vitality of the occasion, there was little life in the game.

The best chance for Ulster to score a try came when Mason sent a pass in the direction of centre Jan Cunningham, who looked to have a clear run to the line, should he catch and gather the ball cleanly. The only problem was, he couldn't see it. The final was Ulster's twentieth European game and Cunningham had missed only one – the first-ever game in the competition to be held at Ravenhill when Bordeaux Bègles had been the visitors. Nobody had started for the side more in Europe, nor indeed scored more tries during the campaign. Beginning with a brace against Morocco all the way back in August, when all of this seemed not just improbable but impossible, Cunningham had crossed the whitewash seven times, including three times in Europe. When Harry Williams first wrote out his projected line-up, Mark McCall had been earmarked for the twelve jersey, but by the time Europe rolled round it was Clinton van Rensburg who started the campaign. With the big South African in Swansea for the quarter-finals, the coach then turned to Stanley McDowell, but his injury ten minutes into the game eventually saw Cunningham get his turn in midfield. This position for Cunningham had been predicted by his Ballymena coach long before, even if not for wholly complimentary reasons. Andre Bester was not a man short on opinions, and on a preseason trip to South Africa he had matter-of-factly told Cunningham that he didn't kick well enough to be a full back and was too slow for the wing. By process of elimination, he became a centre at Eaton Park.

There were less than 240 minutes left of the season when Cunningham made the switch for Ulster, but his understanding with Jonny Bell – displayed in the wins over the two French giants – was a real boost. With the defence employed by Williams dubbed 'the four-up', midfield defence had to be robust, quick and hard-hitting – a style that suited the new pairing.

'Playing in the centre wasn't as big a thing as other people thought,' says Cunningham. 'I was closer to the action and Jonny Bell was brilliant at inside centre. He made it very easy for whoever was playing alongside him. He talked the whole time, he was so organised. I never had to look inside me, Dinger just never ever did the wrong thing.

'We played this four-up blitz defence and other teams hadn't adapted to it. We did it the whole way through the tournament. Stade didn't do well with it, and Toulouse certainly didn't either.'

'Humph and Mark came up with a defensive system where you were playing a flat four,' explains McWhirter. 'That's where that system started. Everyone was playing a drift where you'd have two defenders up, a wing in between and a wing hanging back. It was just a case of everyone into the thirteen. If we could get there quick enough, the ball wouldn't get past thirteen. If we put them under pressure and stopped them before the gain line, then it was me and Wardy in there trying to turn the ball over. It was just pressure – it was almost a rugby league sort of thing.

'The French teams took things at their leisure, but that left them knowing they were in a scrap. We became really hard to score against, and even if you look at the final, Colomiers had enough ball. With that pressure we put on teams, you were going forward and Humph kept the ball ahead of the pack. It's invariably the defensive team that gives away penalties and that's where Simon came in. It was just turning the screw and it rattled teams as well. That structure, and the way it was executed, it was cutting edge. Nobody had tried it then, but it was something they had put together and really looked at. That was one of the reasons that Jan was picked to play thirteen. He was really good defensively and he was durable too. He'd put his head where you wouldn't put your foot.'

Unfortunately it was just that trait that left him with three facial fractures when his moment of glory beckoned. Liz and Lowry Cunningham were both huge influences on their sons Jan and Bryn, as well as on Ross, who by virtue of representing England in touch can claim to be the only international among the brothers. Lowry had played for Queen's during his student days and had a real passion for the game. While he understood the rough and tumble, Liz, who with her husband travelled the length and breadth of Ireland to every game they could, watched almost through her fingers as she prayed her offspring wouldn't sustain any injuries. What happened to Jan in the final was her worst nightmare. The game was only minutes old when Colomiers inside centre, Jérôme Sieurac, took a wide line and looked to slip between Cunningham and Bell. Both men came in to make the tackle, with Cunningham going high to protect against the offload. At the last second, Sieurac ducked his head, which made crushing contact with Cunningham's face. The sickening collision broke his jaw and cheekbone in three places, leaving him with concussion and blurred vision. Somehow he managed to stay in the action, still manning his centre berth when Mason's long pass came towards him and offered an open invite to go down in history as the man who scored the try for Ulster in a European Cup final. With no vision in his left eye, he never had a chance; the dropped ball producing an audible groan from a crowd who had come expecting to witness history.

Unaware of his injury, the match commentary suggested that the occasion had got to the twenty-four-year-old, that nerves on the biggest of stages were to blame for the error on a play he would make in his sleep.

'I just remember a sickening feeling,' says Cunningham of the collision. 'I've no recollection of playing on until half-time at all. I just know I did because I've seen it on video. I'd never have got back on the pitch nowadays. I just remember getting the painkillers and being very upset. It was the right thing, but I was emotional. I don't really remember much until the next day. I didn't really contribute to the game and there was that commentary, "Jan Cunningham, nerves got to him". Not "Jan Cunningham, playing concussed and with a fractured face".

'I suppose you wish it'd never happened but, in some ways, it's one of those things that people remember from the final, that I played for thirty-five minutes with a triple fracture in the face.'

While that try chance went begging, Ulster were certainly getting the better of the decisions and, after Mason knocked over another penalty, Colomiers were incensed that a threatening drive towards the line was halted by the referee's whistle thanks to obstruction. A 10–9 lead at half-time would have had Brunel delivering a very different half-time team talk.

Instead, it was 12–3 to Ulster. Humphreys had been torturing Sadourny all afternoon with an aerial bombardment: the more uncomfortable the French full back looked, the more Ulster's captain would hoist his garryowens skyward to test him. When another was fumbled, the ball was worked off the scrum and, when Colomiers were pinged at the breakdown, Mason banged over his fourth of the game.

At half-time, a somewhat shell-shocked Cunningham caught a glimpse of his eye in the mirror. The decision was made that he couldn't continue and would be replaced by McDowell. The centre hadn't played for Ulster since limping out of the Toulouse quarter-final but had proved his fitness in recent weeks for

Ballymena. His comeback game was for his club's second fifteen, and when restored to All-Ireland League action he impressed in an otherwise lacklustre team performance as a makeshift selection shorn of their Ulster players were beaten heavily by Young Munster just one week before the final. Knowing he was to be thrown into the fray imminently, McDowell had been preparing by getting a final rub-down to help his hamstring through the next forty minutes of action. With the depth of his backline stretched to its very limit, a stressed Williams approached the table and informed McDowell that if he had to come off, he would shoot him.

Williams emphasised to his side that, nine points ahead, the next score was going to be crucial. It came as no surprise, then, that Humphreys was to the fore when it mattered most. In the three minutes after the restart, the out-half produced three kicks: a probing clearance, an inch-perfect up and under and finally a drop goal that kept his side very much on the front foot.

In the play that preceded the three-pointer, it was Bell who got over the ball to steal back possession for his side – the Irish international having one of the games of his life on the biggest stage. Making tackle after tackle, including four in two memorable second-half minutes, defensively-minded Bell was well suited to the contest. He stood out for his determination to bounce back up from the turf and go again.

Like Stade Français before them, Colomiers' only real area of superiority was the scrum, but it gave them little foothold in the game. As their chances of victory became more and more remote, discipline appeared to be optional – one penalty awarded in their favour was even reversed after Patrick Tabacco lashed out, and there were accusations of untoward behaviour, including an unfriendly squeeze of a sensitive area of Rab Irwin's anatomy.

By the time Mickaël Carré hurled the ball into the crowd with frustration after what should have been a score was chalked off for a forward pass, even the most ardent Colomiers supporters had surely accepted it wasn't going to be their day.

Mason's fifth penalty of the afternoon ended the contest after only fifty-three minutes, and what had once seemed impossible now appeared inevitable. Indeed, the last quarter of the game had a surreal feel, with little chance that Colomiers could suddenly spring to life and somehow overhaul a three-score deficit.

Drama had accompanied them all the way through the competition but now, at the very last, there was no tension. For all they'd overcome en route, for all the times it seemed their race was run, it was almost odd that the competition would end this way for Ulster. For months Harry Williams' unfancied outfit had faced make-or-break moments that could have ended their European interest long before that afternoon's final. As the minutes ticked away it was hard not to reflect on all the twists and turns of their most remarkable of journeys: what if the IRFU hadn't decided to bring their exiled internationals home? What if Edinburgh had converted that late overlap in the very first game? What if Toulouse hadn't succumbed at the hands of Ebbw Vale in the biggest shock in the competition's history? What if Sheldon Coulter hadn't slipped into Iain Sinclair's passing lane or if Craig Chalmers hadn't shanked his late penalty? What if Simon Mason hadn't kicked everything within a country mile of the opposition's posts? Would Ulster have bested Stade Français if the venue had been changed from Ravenhill or if Humphreys had kicked for the sideline rather than chipping over an unsuspecting Stade backline? What if, as had looked likely during the summer, the competition hadn't taken place at all?

On the cusp of immortal glory, Humphreys was doing his utmost to ensure his players' heads remained focused on the job at hand until the game was officially in the books. A crying Tony McWhirter had already left the field and been replaced by Derick Topping when Andy Matchett asked his captain how long was left in the game. 'Twelve minutes,' he was told with an air of authority, but in truth there were only seconds. Despite Carré kicking his side's second penalty of the game to double their points tally, Mason stayed perfect with his sixth effort. It felt as though the game could have continued all day and Mason still wouldn't have missed, nor would Colomiers have been able to get any closer than arm's length.

Then, with one final blast of Clayton Thomas's whistle, the most unlikely kings of Europe were crowned.

21
CHAMPIONS

Mark McCall will joke that for a long time he knew more about David Humphreys' father than the man himself.

'We were going down to a game in Munster and we'd ended up saying we'd go down together because his dad was driving,' says the man who, much to his frustration, had enjoyed the best view of all during the historic victory.

'I was walking up to the car and David told me to get in the front which, originally, I thought was nice of him. I got in and looked into the back where this array of blankets and pillows had been laid out for the golden child to sleep all the way down to Limerick. Me and his dad had a good chat at least.'

Despite these somewhat inauspicious beginnings, the two players were firm friends by the time Ulster were crowned European champions, having been teammates for Ulster, London Irish and Ireland for years. Humphreys had been standing beside Andy Ward when the final whistle blew to put Colomiers out of their misery. He was hoisted on to the shoulders of fans who, once again, had emptied the terraces and filled the field in the kind of display that would soon be a relic of the past. As the players drifted towards the trophy presentation, Humphreys searched for his old pal to ensure they would lift the trophy together.

'He was the captain, not me,' says Humphreys matter-of-factly. 'Mark was a big part of winning the European Cup, even though he hadn't played. He'd been such an influential player, it was only right that he was there to be part of that historic moment.'

One key player, however, almost missed lifting the trophy. As fans swarmed round their victorious heroes, some players found it harder than others to force their way through the heaving mass of bodies. For the unfailingly polite flanker Stephen McKinty there was an uncharacteristic need for rudeness when he looked up and realised that the trophy presentation was nearly over. By the time he had pushed, pulled and elbowed his way through the crowd of backslapping supporters, Ulster's top try scorer in that season's competition was the last man to get his hands on the silverware – after the entire squad and each member of the back-room team. Unusually, as well as medals, the victors were presented with tankards to mark their achievement. Some years later, the competition's top scorer, Simon Mason, was horrified to find his daughters were using his to store dog treats.

Back in the relative seclusion of the dressing room, the players were largely silent for a time, each aware of the magnitude of the moment and their scarcely believable successes. In a wider sense, what the triumph meant to their troubled homeland was evident by those partaking in the celebrations. Andy Ward was sharing a joke with Mo Mowlam, while deep in conversation in the doorway were the skipper and Deputy First Minister Seamus Mallon – it was clear that this was no ordinary sporting triumph.

'It doesn't matter whether you're in Northern Ireland, America, South Africa, wherever – sport and politics are inextricably linked, but that's only on a big level, a macro level,' says Humphreys. 'It didn't affect any of us, it didn't add any pressure or anything and we were happy to see all sides represented. We were all very proud of what we did. We were all proud Ulstermen and we all wanted to see Northern Ireland reflected in a positive way.

For a very short period of time, we were the focal point of the sporting landscape here. Whether it was the media in the south or the north, the support was unbelievable. Ulster was coming out of a troubled time politically and we sat as an almost apolitical team. We got support from everyone. That kick-started rugby in Ulster, that one game. It got people in who had never watched it before.'

McCall wasn't the only man to miss the triumph through injury – Jimmy Topping as well as Maurice Field were also unable to play but they were there with the team, celebrating the victory. So too was Willie Anderson, whose own Ulster side had never been given the chance to prove themselves as Europe's best. The giant lock, who as Ireland captain had stared down the haka in this famous old ground ten years before, toasted the team's success with a beer and told the players to enjoy their night before retreating into the background.

If Ulster's triumph defied all odds, it still couldn't enable its assistant coach, Colin Wilkinson, to defy the laws of science. When he tried to enjoy a cigarette away from the media and cameras, he found the only private place was the shower. He enlisted Simon Mason's help, but even the man who could do no wrong struggled to find a way to light a damp Benson & Hedges.

At the reception the always gregarious Wilkinson was handed the microphone to keep the squad entertained … or most of the squad. One player was late, very late, to dinner. Given that it was the same man who describes himself as capable of bringing home gold were talking ever to be made an Olympic sport, it is perhaps no surprise that Mark Blair was caught in conversation. He had been one of the last ready to make his way to the meal. In something of a rush, the lock hadn't heard that when leaving the Berkeley Court for the adjacent Jurys Inn, the players were to take the service exit to avoid the crowds that had already started to gather in the lobby. Following team manager John

Kinnear, who had the European Cup for company, Blair – who was yet to lose in an Ulster jersey – unwittingly took a wrong turn and was thrust into the middle of a raucous crowd. Unsure of the best plan of attack, Kinnear let Blair take the lead.

'It was rammed with people and John thrust the trophy into my hand,' says Blair. 'The next thing everything went quiet. What do you do in that situation? I just stuck the cup in the air and the place erupted. Of course, then you're talking to people forever as you're making your way through. I caught up with the family, talked to all the fans. Everyone was halfway through their food before they even realised I had gone the wrong way.'

Once dinner was finished, players were free to do as they chose. Some were so mentally exhausted that they quickly retreated to bed for a well-earned rest. The others? 'We did what we always did and got absolutely bladdered,' says Mason.

Few, though, did it in as regal a style as Stuart Duncan and Murtagh Rea. When the players had walked into the changing room after concluding their magical season, they were met with cases and cases of champagne. There was the usual spraying and swigging, the type that involved more bubbles going up your nose than in your mouth, but it was quickly apparent that there was too much champagne for even this squad to drink – despite all the celebrations. Duncan had a brainwave. Making sure he left his match jersey in his kit bag, he sacrificed the rest of his gear, no doubt swept up by whatever poor soul was responsible for cleaning up after the celebrations. Filling his bag with as many bottles as possible, he left Lansdowne Road accompanied by the sound of clinking glass. Quite where to drink the champagne, though, was a challenge. Another brainwave: he and Rea, the two battle-scarred Malone men, climbed into one of the carriages drawn by horses that take tourists and romance seekers around St Stephen's Green at night and toasted the victory. When the journey ended and the driver asked what they would like to do, the pair looked down at the bag, still holding a plentiful supply of champagne and replied, 'Go around again, sir.'

Understandably, the next morning came quicker for some than others, but nonetheless all the players were present and correct for the journey back to Belfast. No train travel this time around; instead the players were to return by bus. Harry Williams warned his players to take it easy on the journey north – but the team had serious doubts that anyone would turn up to welcome them home. It seems that Williams may have shared their point of view – his warning quickly forgotten when he produced a bottle of dark rum and passed it round.

There was one quick stop to make on the way home: Dublin Airport. While the pro players, the ones without international commitments at any rate, were months away from their next day's work, Stephen McKinty was due in Chicago on business on Monday morning. He had suggested he would make the journey in a taxi, but Williams gave the idea short shrift: his team would travel together. With the terminal full of expats who had travelled back to Ireland to be part of the historic occasion, it soon became clear that some had been paying greater attention than others. As McKinty queued to check-in for his transatlantic flight, the men behind him were offering various opinions on the game they had witnessed, including who had and hadn't performed well, all blissfully unaware that they were standing next to one of the select few who had helped author the tale.

Another not making the homeward journey was reserve fly half Bryn Cunningham, who had an All-Ireland League game with Bective against Old Belvedere.

'The celebrations were unbelievable, but I had that thing in my head that I was supposed to be playing a game the next day,' he says. 'The guys were heading home and it sounded like it was going to be a bit of a carnival and you were sort of thinking about whether you should get out of the game and join them. But it was a really important game and I felt that it was more important for me to play. I suppose I felt like a wee bit of an outsider with the cup because I'd played so little. I felt an immense sense of pride at being part of it, and I knew that the team had confidence in me and I was made to feel a part of it, but I hadn't earned the plaudits. I didn't play in the final and that left me thinking that I had a job to do for my club and I needed to play. I did and we lost, so I probably should have just joined the party.'

Back on the road the bleary-eyed group, their worsening state not helped by a rule that said they had to drink every time a passing car honked its horn, became increasingly anxious that their Belfast homecoming would be something of a damp squib – that with so many of their fans still in Dublin savouring the last of the weekend, there would be nobody there to welcome them back. By the time they reached their familiar haunt of the Wellington Park, Andy Park required a tactical visit to the bathrooms before the side switched to an open-top bus for the procession through the streets. As they travelled down the Malone Road and on to Great Victoria Street, it seemed as though their worst fears were to be realised. But as the bus prepared to loop round and come up High Street towards City Hall, a glance up Wellington Place revealed thousands of fans lining the route. They had patiently waited for their heroes to arrive, and had been kept up to date on the estimated time of arrival by an official with a loudspeaker. The sight of the bus, and the players on the top deck with the trophy in hand, produced a cheer the like of which hadn't been heard since the final whistle at Lansdowne Road.

Sadly that would be the last of the celebrations for Jan Cunningham. It was decided immediately after the reception that the centre's hugely swollen eye was getting no better and that he should go straight to the Ulster Hospital.

'The boys were living off it for a week, but I missed all that,' he remembers. 'I was in the ward, it was a specialist [ward] for eye surgeries and there were three guys in there with the big bandages over their eyes – three likely lads, shall we say. One of them turns to me and in this thick accent said, "Were you bottled too, mate?"

'I just went "Aye." I didn't want to say "Well, no, actually, I did it playing rugby." Lying in the ward, every time the news came on and had something on the game, I was pulling the sheets over my head.'

For half the squad, the celebrations didn't go on for much longer either because they were scheduled to be on national duty the next week, whether for Ireland or Ireland A. They made their return to Dublin in style after Mike Reid hired limos for them for the journey.

For those still in Belfast the party rolled on, with Sheldon Coulter's birthday on the Monday the perfect excuse for another day's revelry. One local businessman recognised an opportune moment and hired cars to take the players around his string of local bars; the chance to share a pint with the province's newly minted sporting superstars proved popular. When Andy Matchett returned to work on the Thursday after a week away, his bosses were surprised to see him so soon.

After leading their province to such an incredible high, both Humphreys and Mason had less to celebrate in the green jersey. Humphreys, on the same spot he had enjoyed such a triumph the week before, missed a late kick that could have sealed victory over France. Mason was in the stands watching, having somehow been left on the bench for the second string. That Ulster's goal-kicking maestro didn't see action for the A side in Donnybrook was a real disappointment to at least a few in the crowd.

Several of the Ballymena boys – Tony McWhirter, Andy Park, Sheldon Coulter and Andy Matchett –were inspired by Reid's limousine gesture.

'We went bonkers,' recalls McWhirter of the celebrations. 'The season was over, and we were on the hoover for the week. It was only the rabble that were left, the ones that weren't picked for Ireland or Ireland A, and somebody just decided we'd get this limo and go to the A game. We went straight to the Berkeley Court when we got into Dublin, and nobody was out of order. We'd had a few beers but we were all still sensible, and then Noel Murphy the IRFU president came over to say hello.

'He said he had better head to the game and we offered him a lift, so we bring him out and get him in the back of this limo and pull up outside Donnybrook. He's panicking this is going to get caught on a TV camera or something and says "Jesus, lads, I can't be seen getting out of this car with you eejits."

'He made the driver go around the back and sneak him in, then bought us a beer and went off to watch the match. Sometimes you forget these things after a while but then you get together and someone will bring up the time we kidnapped Noisy Murphy.'

22
WHAT NEXT?

Many of the thousands who had descended on Dublin for the final had stayed as close as possible to the scene of Ulster's triumph – some whether they had a hotel reservation or not. So it was no surprise that on the night of 30 January, pubs all over the city were ablaze with talk of just what Ulster's triumph would mean for the team. In one such conversation Allen Clarke told Mike Reid that this was the kind of thing people would still be talking about in twenty years' time, a prophetic observation on his part. The most poignant of all the Guinness-fuelled musings, however, was made to no one in particular. In the centre of The Lincoln's Inn, not far from St Stephen's Green – the location of Stuart Duncan and Murtagh Rea's midnight ride – a twenty-four-year-old student from Belfast took one last sup of his stout and, within earshot of a *Belfast Telegraph* reporter, exclaimed, 'Life can't get any better than this.' He paused before adding, 'What am I to do for the rest of it?'

The question was equally applicable to Ulster. The most surprising of European Cup winners had beaten all comers over the course of their magical five-month run, but they did so as underdogs. Without serious addition to their playing squad, they would be defending their crown with the odds similarly stacked against them. It was a problem that Harry Williams was acutely aware of, even in the hours immediately after his greatest triumph.

'You can talk of new players coming in, or more exiles coming home, but it's going to be hard to surpass this,' he told the journalists gathered in Lansdowne Road. 'Public expectation will be for the same again, which is unlikely.'

The reigning European champions were seen to be on a relatively sound footing come the summer of 1999. While Mark McCall's retirement was official, the drive to return homegrown talent to Ulster had continued. Paddy Johns was back after his deal with Saracens expired, and Tyrone Howe had finally put a serious groin problem behind him, and put his teaching career on hold to sign a professional deal. Three-times capped Irish international Niall Malone, who like Mark Blair before him hadn't represented Ulster before moving across the water, was back home too, after spells with Leicester Tigers and latterly Worcester. With Rab Irwin not offered a new contract, and Gary Leslie still working at Moy Park, the only fully contracted tight head prop on the books was Simon Best. The agriculture student, whose younger brother Rory was already catching the eye as the captain of Portadown College, had been turning out for Newcastle Falcons while at university but agreed to come on board at Ravenhill.

In addition, there were to be new foreign imports and one further Irish international. First capped by Warren Gatland against the nation of his birth in 1998, Dion O'Cuinneagain, the Cape Town native who had family ties to both Dublin and Wexford on his father's side, had seen his contract cancelled by a cash-strapped Sale side and was thought to be deciding between Leinster and Connacht for his move back to his ancestral homeland ahead of Ireland's ill-fated 1999 World Cup campaign. Thanks in no small part to his friendship with Justin Fitzpatrick and Andy Ward, as well as the presence of his compatriot Andre Bester at Ballymena, he instead chose Ulster, boosting a back-row unit that still included Ward, Tony McWhirter and Eric Miller, all on full-time contracts.

Less was known about a globetrotting dreadlocked centre named Riaz Fredericks. He was born in Durban, grew up in Perth and had played representative rugby for Hong Kong before he pitched up in Belfast, having impressed Harry Williams when guesting for North in a Senior Cup game against Portadown shortly before the club merged with Collegians to form Belfast Harlequins. Former England A winger Spencer Bromley was another new recruit, his contract coming at a time when Andy Park was not offered fresh terms.

The last and most exciting of all the fresh faces, though, was Fijian prop Joeli Veitayaki who, unlike Ireland, had impressed at the World Cup. He arrived in November, by which stage Ulster had gone three from six during an interprovincial campaign when they were initially locked out of Ravenhill thanks to improvements required to host Australia versus Romania in the World Cup. With the man mountain having turned down Racing Metro to come to Ulster, there was a palpable buzz in the air when his signing was confirmed, even if the early signs didn't augur well. He was to be unveiled to much fanfare the week between the final two interpros, only to miss his connecting flight from New Zealand, causing the somewhat embarrassing cancellation of a press conference. When he belatedly arrived and was put through a physical by team doctor David Irwin, it was reported in the next day's papers that in response to a question on allergies, he had replied, 'Only McDonalds and KFC.'

Still, as soon as he was able, he was parachuted into the number three jersey for the trip to Bourgoin, where half the town's twenty-thousand-strong population braved the freezing cold temperatures to pack the Stade Pierre Rajon for a chance to see if their hometown heroes could topple the European champions. While only two hundred or so travelling fans made the trip, the game was beamed live to Northern Ireland via the

BBC for locals to see the holders – or at least the seven starters who were left from last year's final – in action against French opposition for the first time since Colomiers had been defeated back in January.

While the performance was actually one of the better they had produced in the campaign, there was little to write home about in the 26–12 defeat. Indeed, despite a controversial try for the hosts, the main talking point had been the performance of Joeli Veitayaki who, after a yellow card, had to be subbed off to prevent the referee sending him off. There were plenty at the time sparing a thought for the side's displaced tight head Rab Irwin who, having been summoned at late notice for a preseason friendly away to Glasgow, felt firmly out of favour from the moment he arrived at the docks for the boat to Stranraer.

With English sides back in the competition, along with named sponsor Heineken, Ulster fared little better against Wasps next time out and lost 19–6. After two games they'd already lost more European encounters than in their victorious campaign. They had the silverware wrenched from their grasp with two defeats at the hands of a Llanelli outfit who had spent their off season investing in the likes of Dafydd James, Patrick Horgan, Craig Gillies and Simon Easterby. When they lost the reverse fixtures against Wasps and Bourgoin, the most horrid of European title defences was complete with a record that read: played six, lost six.

'The fact that it was so bad was hard to deal with at the time,' admits Simon Mason, who along with Tony McWhirter and a revitalised Eric Miller were among the few bright spots of the campaign. 'We needed a few key signings but I don't think even the IRFU were keyed into that at the time. That squad, to kick it on to a level where you could compete regularly, probably needed four or five players. We trained hard, it was a hard preseason, but we came back and I just don't think we had the quality. When you're the champions they want to knock you off, too. It's a different mindset. Once you're on top you have to set the standards higher because everyone wants to take your legs from under you.'

By the time Ulster next won in Europe, some twenty months on from Colomiers, Mason was gone. He'd left Ulster after the 2000 season – as, unsurprisingly, had Fredericks, Bromley and Veitayaki (the former having provided one moment of magic at least with a superb score against Munster) – for a big-money move to the same Stade Français side he had so memorably helped swat aside in 1999.

'It was disappointing that we didn't embrace the opportunity,' Mason says of the break-up of the side that provided the province's greatest day. 'It's not blaming anybody, I just think they'd probably look back and think – could we have got this player, could we have got that player. That group of people had already overachieved. That's a powerful thing. As a teacher I spend my life trying to get people to overachieve, but you have to build on it.'

Ulster couldn't. It would be twelve years before they even got out of their pool again.

EPILOGUE

19 May 2012 – Twickenham Stadium

Ulster may have been the first Irish side to be deemed the kings of Europe, but their storybook win – the vibrancy of which made it all but impossible for the English clubs and the sponsors to maintain their boycotts – was only the beginning. The trail blazed by Mason, Humphreys and Co. was soon followed by the other provinces: Munster reached the final a year later losing a heartbreaker to the Northampton Saints, and fell at the last hurdle again in 2002, this time beaten by Leicester Tigers. They would finally triumph in 2006, beating Biarritz in Cardiff, before repeating the feat against Toulouse two years later. Not long after, Leinster were the Heineken Cup's dominant force, winning two of the three titles prior to booking their place in the 2012 final. That year, Irish monopolisation of the competition reached its zenith with Ulster taking the other spot.

Ulster's run to the Twickenham showpiece hadn't quite matched the thrills and spills of the 1998–99 campaign – what could? – but there was no denying that emerging from a pool with Clermont and Leicester Tigers was an impressive feat, let alone beating Munster at Thomond Park in the last eight.

With eighty-two thousand in attendance, everywhere you

looked were reminders of how the game had changed since Ulster were last the pride of the continent. The idea of players pleading for time off work to train is laughable; the thought of half the squad making a five-hundred-mile round trip for an All-Ireland League match as their preparation would have been enough to give a coach a coronary.

Links to 1999, however, remained plentiful; the inspiration provided by that unforgettable success evident in the men who took to the old Cabbage Patch hoping to emulate the feat.

Paddy Wallace, the team's inside centre and the province's record appearance maker, was on the very edge of the 1999 squad. In his first year out of school, he had trained with the senior panel in the preseason before heading to Dublin to study. He'd returned home to watch the Toulouse and Stade Français games and had made the short jaunt from his flat just off Pearse Street to Lansdowne Road for the final before playing for UCD against Terenure the next day. Ten years on he'd been on the field for a different piece of history, Ireland's first Grand Slam since 1948.

Like starting openside Chris Henry, Wallace's midfield partner, Darren Cave was also in the stands thirteen years earlier, a ten-year-old attending with his father and older brother. Together he and Wallace were charged with negating the impact of Brian O'Driscoll and Gordon D'Arcy, the duo who went from training with the Ireland squad for the first time the month Simon Mason kicked Colomiers' dream to pieces to become the nation's best-ever centre pairing.

The large influx of world-class foreign talent was brought to Belfast by none other than David Humphreys who – after retiring from the game, having delivered Ulster the Celtic League title with a late drop goal that bounced off both posts – became the province's first operations manager in the summer of 2008. His appointment was an acknowledgement by Mike Reid that the game had moved on, that he himself could no longer attract the type of players required for the side to have any impact on

Europe. Among Humphreys' first batch of signings were a trio of World Cup winners: the All Blacks tight head John Afoa and the Springboks duo of Ruan Pienaar and Johann Muller.

'We had to stop trying to get the Joeli Veitayakis of this world and go get the Pienaars and the Mullers,' says Reid. 'I knew I couldn't do that, so I appointed David. To me it was obvious – he was a very good leader of people, like Harry Williams in that way. He's a non-drinker, a family man, but he's hugely respected in the game. I got stick for it because he was well paid but we had gone through lean years and I thought he was the right person to get us out of it.'

Like Harry Williams, Brian McLaughlin, the coach Humphreys worked alongside, was a retired school teacher, while Jonny Bell, man of the match in the 1999 final, was on the ticket, too, as a defensive specialist. Of the local lads pulling on the white jersey in the plush surrounds of west London, a third of them came through the academy during former lock Gary Longwell's spell as manager, while it was Allen Clarke who first convinced the mother of Lions flanker Stephen Ferris that her son had a big future in the game.

Plenty of those not still directly involved in the game were in Twickenham to watch, chief among them Simon Mason, who desperately wanted to see the side equal his own achievement.

'I'd be the first to say that pound for pound we weren't as good a team as the one from 2012,' he admits. 'For me, I've always wanted to see them do it again but every year it gets harder. I just wouldn't want some of the players now to be sat there thinking, "Aww, I've to live up to those idiots from '99."

'It's a bit like the way some people view being a Liverpool fan – that idea that you shouldn't talk about 1990 just because it hasn't happened since. Every time an Ulster player comes in, it's not like they should be looking at it like a millstone or something.

'It's more embracing the history of what we are. That, for me, is the key thing. It's feeling like you're part of something.

I still watch all the games now nearly twenty years on, and I'd love to see them win it again. I'm sure there's Liverpool players from 1990 who are the same – you take no pleasure in being the last or whatever. The longer it goes, you probably appreciate how it does take a lot of things coming together, all that luck. I mean, if that ball doesn't bounce for Humphs against Stade, we probably don't win, do we? You can put all the hours in you want, you can be this all-singing professional outfit, but you still need something to go your way.'

In Twickenham, nothing bar the first points of the day went the way of the northern province. Just as there was a belief among some players that Ulster couldn't have lost in 1999, on that day Leinster felt they'd won the game before it even began. O'Driscoll watched Ulster in the last eight doing laps of honour around Thomond, smirking at the specially embroidered jerseys they wore in the semi-final win over Edinburgh. He saw a side much like his own before they developed a winning habit. Having managed to do what Ulster couldn't – turning their maiden triumph into a dynasty – they'd already learnt the hard way that just getting there counts for little unless you're hoisting silverware into the sky when the game is over.

In truth, Ulster could be at the peak of their powers and still be forced to stomach the sight of the trophy ending up in Dublin. Leinster boast what will later be looked at as a historically strong team and, while Ulster are able to notionally stay in the game early on, Leinster end it by mowing through their northern neighbours like a chainsaw through butter – the game breaking a plethora of records for a European final: biggest winning margin, most points, most tries … Leinster had proven just far too good.

For now, Ulster's heroes of 1999 still stand alone.

ULSTER RUGBY 1998-99

Name	Position	Played	Tries	Conversions	Penalties	Drop Goals
Simon Mason	Full back	17	3	36	48	1
David Humphreys	Out-half	17	5	-	-	6
Gary Leslie	Prop	17	1	-	-	-
Justin Fitzpatrick	Prop	17	-	-	-	-
Gary Longwell	Lock	17	-	-	-	-
Tony McWhirter	Number 8	17	3	-	-	-
Andy Ward	Flanker	16	5	-	-	-
Jan Cunningham	Wing/Centre	16	6	-	-	-
Allen Clarke	Hooker	16	1	-	-	-
Stephen McKinty	Flanker	15	5	-	-	-
Robert Irwin	Prop	15	-	-	-	-
Jonathan Bell	Centre	14	1	-	-	-
Andrew Matchett	Scrum half	13	2	-	-	-
Sheldon Coulter	Wing/Centre	13	1	-	-	-
Andy Park	Wing	11	2	-	-	-
Stephen Bell	Scrum half	10	3	-	-	-
Mark Blair	Lock	10	2	-	-	-

Name	Position	Played	Tries	Conversions	Penalties	Drop Goals
Stuart Duncan	Flanker	10	-	-	-	-
Murtagh Rea	Lock	9	2	-	-	-
Stanley McDowell	Centre/ Wing	8	2	-	-	-
Clinton van Rensburg	Centre	8	1	-	-	-
Ritchie Weir	Hooker	7	-	-	-	-
Dean McCartney	Flanker	7	-	-	-	-
Derick Topping	Flanker	5	-	-	-	-
Mark McCall	Centre	4	-	-	-	-
Jonathan Davis	Wing	3	-	-	-	-
Bryn Cunningham	Out-half	3	-	-	-	-
James Topping	Winger	1	1	-	-	-
Chris McCarey	Number 8	1	-	-	-	-
Eric Miller	Number 8	1	-	-	-	-

THE STAFF

Harry Williams – Head Coach

Colin Wilkinson – Assistant Coach

David Irwin – Team Doctor

Mike Reid – Chief Executive

Willie Wallace – Bag Man

John Martin – Physio

John Callaghan – Ulster Branch President

WHAT THEY DID NEXT

Simon Mason
Left Ulster for Stade Français in 2000. His career also took in a spell with Italian side Treviso. Retired without adding to his two Ireland caps. Became a teacher in Liverpool and was still turning out for local side Birkenhead Park well into his forties where he let his backline colleagues kick goals.

Sheldon Coulter
His last game for Ulster came in 2003, although he went on to play for Belfast Harlequins, CIYMS and Portadown. Became a financial adviser and remained a regular attendee at Ravenhill.

Jan Cunningham
Played with Ulster until the end of the 2002–03 campaign and, after the conclusion of his pro career, continued to represent Dungannon, captaining the Stevenson Park side. Became a partner in Millar McCall Wylie Solicitors, specialising in employment.

Jonathan Bell
Represented Ireland at the 1999 World Cup, winning the last of his thirty-six caps in the summer of 2003. A stalwart in the Ulster midfield until 2006, he became Elite Player Development Officer at the Ulster Rugby Academy before moving up to work with the senior side as defence coach. Took up the same role with Gloucester in the summer of 2015.

Andy Park
The European Cup-winning campaign was his only as a pro with Ulster but he continued to play his club rugby with North, who became Belfast Harlequins after a merger with Collegians. Worked as an account executive before moving into player

management, representing the likes of British and Irish Lion Iain Henderson.

David Humphreys

Was still the central figure when Ulster won their next piece of major silverware, knocking over a dramatic drop goal that bounced off both posts to secure the Celtic League title in 2006. Retired in 2008 as the most capped Ulsterman of all time. That summer, he became Ulster's Operations Director (later Director of Rugby) and set about assembling the next Ulster team that would challenge for European honours, guiding the side to quarter-finals in 2011, 2013 and 2014, as well as the final in 2012. Left to become Director of Rugby at Gloucester in 2014, taking the cherry and whites to three European Challenge Cup finals in four years, winning the competition in 2015. Awarded an MBE in 2004 for services to rugby.

Andrew Matchett

Was another whose Ulster outings were limited after the 1999 European triumph as the province put even more onus on full-time players. Continued to work for Clerical Medical.

Justin Fitzpatrick

Left Ulster to play for Castres in 2003, spending two years in France where he picked up a Coupe de France winners' medal. Returned to Ravenhill in time to play a part in the Celtic League win of 2006. Played for Ireland at the 1999 World Cup, winning the last of his twenty-six caps in 2003. Injury forced his retirement in 2010. Became coach of Dungannon, bringing both the Senior Cup and Senior League titles back to Stevenson Park in 2011. Was an assistant coach for the US Eagles at the 2015 World Cup and was named the inaugural coach of the Houston SaberCats in 2017.

Allen Clarke

Injury forced his retirement in 2001. As Elite Player Development Manager he established the Ulster Rugby Academy before serving as assistant coach in the Celtic League-winning campaign of 2006. Became High Performance Manager with the IRFU in 2007 and was responsible for revamping Irish Rugby's age-grade structure. Became Elite Performance Manager at Ulster in 2012 before becoming forwards coach in 2014. Left for Ospreys in 2017, where he was named head coach in 2018.

Rab Irwin

The European final would be his last game as a professional rugby player, although he was still called upon the next season. Returned to the building trade and CIYMS. In later years, could still be seen turning out for Ards RFC 4th XV as he neared his fifty-fifth birthday.

Mark Blair

Played for Ulster until 2003 and represented both Narbonne and Borders before ultimately hanging up his boots in 2006. Worked in property development before returning to rugby to act as Development Manager for the Irish Exiles, working to identify Irish-qualified rugby players outside of Ireland. Left the role in the summer of 2017 and founded his own business, Transition Sport. Lives in Edinburgh.

Gary Longwell

After the European success, he won his first Ireland cap in November 2000 at the age of twenty-nine. His twenty-sixth and final time in the green jersey came against Italy in 2004. Surpassed Willie Anderson's Ulster appearance record and became the first man to hit a century of games for the province, ultimately retiring with 152 in 2005. Was High Performance Manager for the Ulster Rugby Academy at a time when the likes of British and Irish Lions Tommy Seymour and Iain Henderson came through the system. Took up the position of Performance Skills Coach at the Sports Institute of Northern Ireland in 2013, working with, amongst others, the Ireland women's hockey squad that reached the World Cup final in 2018.

Stephen McKinty
Called upon only in emergencies after the 1998–99 season as he continued his career with FG Wilson where he ultimately became a General Manager. Continued to play rugby for his beloved Bangor.

Andy Ward
Went on to captain Ulster before retiring in 2005. Represented Ireland at the 1999 World Cup, winning the last of his twenty-eight caps in a victory over France in 2001. As well as continuing to play for Ballynahinch, after his Ulster days were over he coached at Belfast Harlequins and Cooke. Established a successful chain of gyms and worked as a television pundit for BBC Northern Ireland.

Tony McWhirter
A hand injury in 2004 forced him into rugby retirement when he was twenty-nine having made ninety-four appearances for Ulster. Began working in dentistry in Ballymoney and for BBC Northern Ireland as an analyst and commentator.

***

Stan McDowell (for Cunningham, 40)
After a stint as an estate agent, he became coach of the Ireland Sevens team, working with his old Ulster teammate James Topping.

Derick Topping (for McWhirter, 73)
Named captain of Ballymena, continued to work as a medical rep.

Gary Leslie (for Irwin, 73)
The only player to feature in Ulster's first twenty-one European games, culminating in the 1999 final. Continued at Moy Park after playing his last game for Dungannon in 2004.

***

Harry Williams
Left Ulster for a second time in 2001, spending his retirement with his wife in Groomsport.

Mark McCall
Succeeded Alan Solomons as Ulster's head coach in 2004, winning the Celtic League in 2006. However, he left less than eighteen months later. After a spell as an assistant at Castres, he arrived at Saracens in 2010 and became Director of Rugby in 2011. The 2018 Premiership title was his fourth with the Barnet club, while he led them to Europe's top prize in both 2016 and 2017.

ACKNOWLEDGEMENTS

If it takes a village to raise a child, the last year has left me in no doubt that it takes, at the very least, a small army to write a book, and I'm now indebted to so many people that I'm petrified of forgetting one of them!

Like all my best, and admittedly worst, ideas, the one for this book came to me in the Errigle, with Paddy Maguire the first person to agree that it was worth pursuing. Given how many projects that have been discussed around that same table have subsequently bitten the dust, his encouragement was always vital. Having decided that I should write this book, it was my colleague and friend Declan Bogue who told me how, and his advice throughout has been invaluable. The team at Blackstaff Press were equally supportive during the whole process, with Patsy Horton and Helen Wright first hearing my pitch and being there every step of the way thereafter, including ensuring that the ever-thorough Victoria Woodside edited the text. Her stellar efforts ensured that more than one embarrassing error didn't make it through.

Obviously writing this book without the cooperation of the 1998–99 squad would have been impossible, and with every interview request I was amazed at how generous they were with their time. When speaking about the 1999 team the phrase 'a great group of lads' is invariably used and it couldn't be more apt – each interview was a heck of a way to spend an afternoon. In a project like this, tracking people down can initially feel daunting. In this regard, Simon Mason and Stuart Duncan were of great assistance, as were Rod Nawn, Phillip Coulter, Sam O'Byrne, Ian Wallace, Neil Workman and Bill Wallace.

On occasion, though, things just break your way and Stephen McKinty walks into the coffee shop where you're interviewing Andy Matchett.

Thanks also to the *Belfast Telegraph* and to its editor Gail Walker for allowing me to undertake the work to bring this book to fruition and, of course, the opportunity to write about Ulster Rugby in the first place. Jim Gracey offering me six weeks of work experience fresh out of university was the most important moment of my professional life. Without the chance to learn from a sports desk that then included Steven Beacom, Niall Crozier, Billy Weir, David Kelly, Graham Luney, Frank Brownlow, Stuart McKinley and Chris Holt, I'd almost certainly be doing something else for a living – a thought that doesn't bear thinking about for a man whose only experience of a true nine-to-five did not go well, to put it mildly. It's always been a real privilege to cover my local team for my local paper; the same newspaper that landed on our doorstep every afternoon as far back into my childhood as I can remember.

In a city full of them, the Newspaper Library is one of Belfast's hidden gems and its resources and staff were a huge help in producing this book. It was there that I pored over the reports of my *Belfast Telegraph* predecessor Jim Stokes. Articles by Gerry Thornley, Brendan Fanning – as well as his brilliant book *From There to Here* – Peter O'Reilly, Kieran Rooney, Michael Sadlier, John O'Sullivan, John Laverty, Gavin Mairs, Gail Walker, Ciaran Donaghy and Richard Bullick also proved especially useful, as did Bruce McKendry's *Champions*, released in the immediate aftermath of the 1999 triumph.

On the subject of resources, Kyle McNeely's knowledge is something I rely upon far more than I'd care to admit.

My family are the most important people in anything I do, and once again I'm eternally grateful for them. The use of their kitchen table seemed to have me at my most productive … probably something to do with the steady flow of coffee. My poor sister Laura has already read this book more times than anyone else ever will. My propensity for overly lengthy sentences continues to amaze and astound her in equal measure. While there are so many people without whom I couldn't have written this book, endless gratitude goes to Christina, without whom it's always been suspected I wouldn't achieve much of anything at all.

Finally, thanks to anyone and everyone who took the time to bring me to a game.

INDEX

NAMES AND PLACES